The American Bicycle Atlas

American Youth Hostels, Inc.

THE
AMERICAN
BICYCLE
ATLAS

Written and edited by Dave Gilbert

Maps by Dave Gilbert

E. P. Dutton || New York

Published in the United States by Elsevier-Dutton Publishing Co., Inc.,
2 Park Avenue, New York, N.Y. 10016

Library of Congress Catalog Card Number: 80-68799

ISBN: 0-525-93172-4

Published simultaneously in Canada by
Clarke, Irwin & Company Limited, Toronto and Vancouver

Designed by Kingsley Parker

10 9 8 7 6 5 4 3 2 1

First Edition

Acknowledgments

The author extends his warmest thanks to the following people who made this edition of *The American Bicycle Atlas* possible: Tom Newman, Executive Director of American Youth Hostels; Sandra Soule, Editorial Consultant for Travel at E. P. Dutton; Bob Johnson and Bill Nelson of American Youth Hostels; Dave French of the Potomac Area Council–AYH; Dick Wilhelm for his many tour contributions; Greg Siple, who will forever be remembered for TOSRV; A. Virginia Phelan of the League of American Wheelmen; Bruce Burgess for his compilation of bicycle trail guides; John Mosley; Jay Martin Anderson; and Dave Perka for his timely and helpful comments on my introductory chapters.

I would also like to thank the following people who contributed tours for this *Atlas:*

NORTHEAST

Debbie Barlow, *Vermont Dept. of Forests, Parks & Recreation*
Richard Cohen, *Manter Memorial Youth Hostel*
Charles H. Dane, *Massachusetts Dept. of Environmental Management*
Joseph G. Dias, *Rhode Island Dept. of Environmental Management*
Ron Gallagher, *Greater Boston Council—AYH*
D. Goodale, *Train Hostel*
Martha Guthridge, *Ski Hostel Lodge Youth Hostel*
New York Office of Parks & Recreation
George Plumb, *Vermont Dept. of Forests, Park & Recreation*
Rhode Island Dept. of Economic Development

Robert Schiff
Nancy Jean Steffen
Howard Stone
Martin & Anne Vesenka, *Friendly Crossways Youth Hostel*

MID-ATLANTIC

Robert Bushnell, *Maryland Dept. of Natural Resources*
Paul Evans
Gettysburg National Military Park
Donna Purcell Mayes, *Virginia Dept. of Highways &
    Transportation*
Louis A. Rodia, *New Jersey Dept. of Public Affairs*

SOUTHEAST

Bob Meader
Richard Nave
George Rapier, Jr., *Pensacola Freewheelers Bicycle Club*
Maxwell S. Sanders, *Natchez Trace Parkway*

MIDWEST & GREAT LAKES

Laura J. Black, *Illinois Office of Tourism*
Kim Dammers
Ed Honton, *Columbus Council—AYH*
Terry Maurer, *Bluegrass Area Development District*
Richard Nave
G. Neal Overbey, *Indiana Dept. of Natural Resources*
Parke County Tourist Information Center
Martin Rabb
Sue Reichardt, *Ozark Area Council—AYH*
Marvin Watson, *Michigan Dept. of Natural Resources*

NORTHERN PLAINS

Don Andrews
Minnesota Council—AYH
Gerri Thorsteinson

SOUTHERN PLAINS

Sara Burroughs
Larry Christie
Marietta Diehl
Jay S. Miller, *Arkansas Trails Council*
Sue Reichardt, *Ozark Area Council—AYH*
Mark Widder

NORTHWEST

Stuart Crook, *Bikecentennial*
Mrs. Gene Hibbard, *Washington State Council—AYH*
Josh Lehman, *Seattle Engineering Dept.*
H. Sangster, *Salem Bicycle Club*
T. N. Townley, *Washington Dept. of Transportation*
Ev Woodward, *Lodge Youth Hostel*

SOUTHWEST

Jan Blevins
Donald S. Bliss, *League of American Wheelmen*
Mary Cosaboom, *Central Arizona Bicycling Association*
Bruce Leaf and Mike Ebbs, *The Spoke, Ltd.*
Lou Livingston, *Rocky Mountain Council—AYH*
Jay Meierdierck, *Nevada State Parks*

CALIFORNIA

Caltrans, District 1
Emmett Chalk, *Caltrans, District 10*
Clifford Graves, *International Bicycle Touring Society*
Herbert Greenberg, *Santa Rosa Cycling Club*
Jay Meierdierck, *Nevada State Parks*
Hal Munn, *Los Angeles Wheelmen*
Willmot White, *Caltrans, District 4*

Credits

#16, #17, #18: *North Country Bike Routes*, by New York Office of Parks & Recreation.

#32: *A Guide to Recreational Bicycling in Albemarle County*, by Paul Evans.

#39: *Biking Western Michigan*, by Michigan Dept. of Natural Resources.

#43, #44, #45: Columbus Council of American Youth Hostels.

#46: text by Greg Siple.

#47: *Hoosier Hills Route*, by Indiana Dept. of Natural Resources.

#51, #52, #60: *Bicycle Tours, Greater St. Louis Area*, by Ozark Area Council—AYH.

#57, #58: *Minnesota Bike Atlas*, by Minnesota Council—AYH.

#61: *Kansas Bicycle Routes*, by Biking Across Kansas.

#71: *Trans-America Trail, Coast-Cascades*, by Bikecentennial.

#72: *Bicycling Thru the Evergreen State*, by Washington State Dept. of Transportation.

#82: *Bicycle Touring*, by The Spoke, Ltd., Boulder, CO.

Table of Contents

Preface

ABOUT HOSTELING

Hosteling is a special experience. It is being on your own, self-propelled and self-sufficient. It is meeting people—all kinds of people from all over the world—and helping them to understand you as you learn to understand them. Hosteling is a ticket to the adventure of exploring a bit of the world firsthand, and getting to know yourself.

Hostels are low-cost travel accommodations where you can sleep and eat inexpensively. Most hostels have separate men's and women's dormitories with double-deck bunks. Hostels provide bathroom facilities, usually a fully equipped kitchen where you can prepare your own meals, and a common room where hostelers can meet at the end of the day and share their special adventures. Generally, overnight fees at hostels range from $3 to $6. Alcohol and drugs are not permitted, and smoking is permitted only in designated areas. Visits are usually limited to three days.

In North America, a hostel may be a college dormitory, an old farm, a mountain lodge, a restored railroad car, an old jail, or even a restored lifeguard station on an Atlantic beach. Today, there are over 240 hostels in the United States, and some 5,000 hostels in fifty member countries of the International Youth Hostel Federation worldwide. Hostel users must be members of the American Youth Hostels (AYH) or of the International Youth Hostel Federation (IYHF), and there are no age restrictions for joining. Individual, family, and group memberships are available. Foreign visitors who do not hold a card issued by their home country can purchase an

International Guest Card (Foreign National Card) for use in the United States.

Founded in 1934, the purpose of American Youth Hostels is to help all people, especially young people, gain a greater understanding of the world and its people through outdoor activities, educational and recreational travel, and service programs; to develop fit, self-reliant, well-informed citizens; and to provide hostels in scenic, historic, and cultural areas. AYH is a nonprofit organization supported by memberships, program fees, and voluntary contributions.

For more information, contact your local AYH council (listed under *National Bicycling Organizations & AYH Councils* in Chapter 3) or write *American Youth Hostels, National Organization, 1332 "I" St., NW, 8th Floor, Washington, DC 20005*. For information on Canadian hostels, write *Canadian Hosteling Association, 333 River Road, Vanier City, Ottawa, Ontario, Canada K1L 8B9*.

ABOUT THE AUTHOR

Dave Gilbert has been active in hosteling for the past ten years. As a teen-ager he spent five weeks cycling with AYH in the Canadian Rockies. As an adult he has led several summer trips for the Potomac Area Council—AYH, has directed their summer travel program, and has served as that Council's executive director. A graduate of the University of Virginia in 1975, Dave has also edited the *Greater Washington Area Bicycle Atlas* and has written *Rivers & Trails*, a guide to outdoor travel in the mid-Atlantic states. Dave is currently houseparent at the Kiwanis Hostel in Sandy Hook, Maryland, where he completed work on this book.

PART ONE

Cycling Information

THE DANDY-HORSE

A Curious Invention.—In *Ackerman's Magazine* for this month (Feb., 1819) is an account of a machine denominated the pedestrian hobby-horse. Invented by a Baron von Drais, a gentleman at the court of the Grand Duke of Baden, and which has been introduced into this country by a tradesman in Long Acre. The principle of this invention is taken from the art of skating, and consists in the simple idea of a seat upon two wheels, propelled by the feet acting upon the ground. The riding-seat, or saddle, is fixed on a perch upon two double-shod wheels running after each other, so that they can go upon the footways. To preserve the balance, a small board, covered and stuffed, is placed before, on which the arms are laid, and in front of which is a little guiding-pole, which is held in the hand to direct the route. The swiftness with which a person well practised can travel is almost beyond belief—eight, nine, and even ten miles may, it is asserted, be passed over within the hour on good level ground. The machine, it is conjectured, will answer well for messengers, and even for long journeys; it does not weigh more than 50 pounds, and may be made with travelling pockets.

From a contemporary newspaper

CHAPTER ONE
About Bicycle Touring

INTRODUCTION

The bicycle is a remarkable machine, a simple tool that converts the expense of human energy into forward motion in the most efficient manner known. It emits no exhaust, makes no noise, consumes no fuel, and generally improves the health of its operator. The two-wheeler affords flexibility in travel distance—anywhere from ten to one hundred miles are possible in a given day—without sacrificing the roadside convenience of stores, hostels, and that occasional frosty ice cream cone. Doing away with the steel and glass envelope created by the automobile, the bicycle keeps you in close touch with the land. Roadside wild flowers come into focus, birds sing in magnificent chorus, and sweet corn ripens under your very nose. By adding a tent, sleeping bag, and toothbrush to your rear carrier, you can extend your range and attain an exhilarating dimension of self-sufficiency.

In amazing numbers, Americans are coming to grips with the bicycle. Since first being introduced into this country during the Centennial Exposition of 1876, inventors have steadily improved upon the European model. Transportation pioneers Henry Ford, Glenn Olds, and Orville and Wilbur Wright all dabbled first in the development of the two-wheeler. With the introduction of the ten-speed "English racer" in the 1960s, sales boomed. From 1970 to 1979, some 77 million bicycles were sold in the United States alone—a million more than passenger cars sold during the same period. Today, the Bicycle Manufacturers Association estimates that over 100 million Americans ride their bicycles at least occasionally.

3

As a family endeavor, a bicycle tour is a perfect way to get both parents and children involved in a trip. Rather than drawing up lines of battle between the front and rear seats of your car, a family outing by bicycle is a perfect way to spend the day. Your kids suddenly have a responsibility for their own performance, a specific goal to work for, and an accomplished feat to take pride in. And what better way is there to wear out your kids by bedtime! If your children are still toddlers, they can be placed in one of several small seats designed to safely hold the child on the back of your bicycle. It beats paying for a baby-sitter, and is certainly more entertaining for you and your child.

Can your kids endure the physical challenge? Don't sell them short. During the summer of 1976, on a series of long-distance bicycle tours sponsored by a national bicycling organization, participants ranged in age from seven to eighty-six. Two nine-year-olds completed an entire coast-to-coast trip.

Compiled both to inform and to guide, *The American Bicycle Atlas* tackles questions of safe and intelligent bicycle use, presents source information for bicycle tourists, and describes bicycle trips from coast to coast. We want to get you out on your bicycle, whether for an hour-long ride in a scenic city park, for a day-long trip in the country, or for a week-long tour in a distant part of America. While our goal is to provide every cyclist with accurate and reliable information on biking in America, mistakes are inevitable, and we welcome your comments and corrections.

CHOOSING A BICYCLE

With so many models and brand names of bicycles to choose from, where do you start? First, consider the bike's utility and your individual needs. Is the model appropriate for commuting, racing, day tripping, extended touring, or some combination of these categories? Second, consider cost. With new bicycles ranging in price from $60 to $2,000, it is easy to be hustled onto a model that's not right for you.

Models. The single-speed balloon tire bomber is a relatively inexpensive bicycle with foot brakes. Ranging in cost from $60 to $150, this model is suitable for any rider who plans to travel on rough roads or doesn't want to deal with flat tires and fussy gearshifts. This bike is particularly appropriate for local city commuting, cycling at beach resorts, and for riding on old canal towpaths and converted railroad right-of-ways. The wide tires and single gear, however, make this bicycle undesirable for long-distance travel.

The classic three-speed bicycle gives you a strong, heavy frame with a choice of gears. Total weight ranges from 35 to 50 pounds, and prices vary from $80 to $170. Climbs are made easier, but the upright position of the rider becomes uncomfortable on longer rides. This model is appropriate for commuting and for occasional day-trips in the country.

The ten-speed bicycle is the most popular choice of adult enthusiasts. This bike is generally lightweight (20 to 40 pounds) and offers a wide range of gears that make travel over varied terrain easier. The dropped handlebars put the cyclist in the most efficient position to deliver power to the pedals, improve overall weight distribution, and lessen wind resistance. This results in a minimum of fatigue on long rides. Prices range from $100 for heavier models with steel components to about $2,000 for a top-of-the-line racing bike. Models between $200 and $400 are appropriate for general long-distance touring, offering quality frame tubing and lugged frame construction, durable alloy components, and less overall weight.

A tandem model accommodates two cyclists at the same time. This model offers dropped handlebars, five to fifteen speeds, and the same quality components available on many ten-speed models. A tandem is appropriate for a married couple, parent and child, or cycling partners who enjoy working together. Due to the increased weight of two riders, durability and stopping power are very important. Look for a model with heavy-duty wheels and front and rear brakes. Expect to pay anywhere from $400 up to $1,500 for a lightweight touring model with alloy wheels.

Frames. After you have decided on an appropriate model, make sure the particular machine you are looking at fits you. To size the bicycle, straddle the frame with both feet flat on the floor. You should not be able to lift the bike more than an inch off the floor.

We recommend a "men's" (or diamond) frame for both men and women. The frame design on most "women's" bikes is generally weaker than the standard diamond frame. A compromise is the "mixte" frame, a cross between a diamond frame and a woman's frame which is quite strong and durable.

Inspect the frame. Are the tube joints tight and free from defects? Generally, bicycle frames are made with either lugged or lugless (brazed) joints. A lug is a sleeve into which a tube fits. A lugged frame is generally stiffer than a brazed frame. It absorbs road shocks well and transmits the energy of pedaling more efficiently into forward motion. With lugless frames, energy tends to be lost in the flexing of the frame during the action of pedaling. Lugless frames do generally cost less, and use a heavier gauge of mild steel tubing to compensate for the loss of strength at the brazed joints.

Expect to pay more for an alloy frame. An alloy is two or more metals mixed together, resulting in a stronger overall metal per ounce. The strength of alloy permits frame tube walls to be thinner and consequently lighter. Like a compact car, a lighter bike will get better "gas" mileage; that is, more miles for the amount of energy exerted by the cyclist.

Components. Most bicycles come equipped with clincher tires— tires with a separate inner tube that can be removed. Clinchers are more durable for general touring, are much easier to repair, and are available in high-pressure models which reduce road friction for better "gas" mileage. Some bicycles offer tubular (or sew-up) tires—tires with an inner tube sewn into the outer tire. Tubulars are generally designed for racing, take more time to repair (unless you pack spares), and cost from $20 to $35 for a single tire. Clinchers and sew-ups can be used on the same bike, but must be fit with different rims.

Leather seats are your best bet for the money. They usually take a season to break in, but will last you a long time. Molded (or anatomic) saddles consist of a nylon base with a leather cover. Molded saddles are designed for the anatomy of either sex, and are recommended for women in particular since standard leather saddles are designed for a man's anatomy.

When choosing brakes, you will find that center-pull brakes are your best bargain. Center-pulls provide excellent stopping power, but your brake levers will usually have a spongy feel when you apply them. High-quality side-pull brakes have a much firmer feel when you apply them, have fewer moving parts, are simpler to adjust, and provide stopping power equal to that of center-pulls. Side-pull brakes are generally more expensive also.

Avoid brake extension levers which allow braking from the top of the handlebars. They generally do not permit firm braking for quick stops, and put your center of gravity in a dangerously high position for a quick stop situation.

If you plan to do a lot of bicycle commuting in all types of weather, fenders are useful for deflecting water and dirt tossed up by your wheels. A kickstand is useful when commuting or day riding, but will not hold up a bicycle loaded with saddlebags and camping gear. In the latter case, Flickstands are available which lock your front wheel in the straight position, allowing you to lean your loaded bicycle upright against a tree or pole.

Toe clips are desirable on day trips and longer tours. They keep the ball of your foot centered over the pedal for the efficient application of power, keep your foot from slipping off the pedal, and permit "ankling." While one foot pushes down on the pedal, the other foot pulls up, allowing you to get the most from each revolution of the pedal.

Adjustments. Several simple adjustments should be made before you ride your bicycle. First, raise or lower the seat to a position where, sitting on the saddle and resting the ball of your foot on the pedal at its lowest position, you have only a slight bend at the knee. The saddle should either have no tilt or only a very slight forward tilt. The handlebars should then be adjusted to the same level as the front of the saddle. Both the seat post and handlebar stem should extend at least two inches into the frame tubes. Place your elbow at the front point of the saddle and extend your forearm toward the handlebars. Your fingertips should just rest on top of the handlebar stem. Adjust your saddle forward or backward accordingly.

Grip the brake levers and check the contact between the brake pads and wheel. The brake pads should grip the metal rim firmly and squarely. They should not make contact with the tire. Adjust the front and rear derailleur, if necessary, after you've ridden the bicycle. Small adjustment screws are provided on both mechanisms.

BICYCLE REPAIR

Keeping your bicycle in good running order makes sense. If you can perform regular maintenance and basic repairs yourself, you'll avoid costly visits to the bike shop and spare yourself the inconvenience of being stuck on a country road with a flat tire or a broken gear cable.

You don't need to know everything, but do learn to deal with the more likely road repairs: fixing a flat tire, adjusting loose break pads, replacing broken cables, adjusting front and rear derailleur assemblies, and, in extreme cases, replacing a broken spoke. Even emergency remedies that will get you to a bike shop, such as stuffing hay in a flat tire or wiring together a broken component, are appropriate in some cases.

Oil moving parts occasionally to insure smooth operation. Just a drop or two on the front and rear derailleur is sufficient. Oil the chain sparingly if needed. The springs or hinges on your brakes might also need an occasional drop or two of oil.

To learn the basics, take a bicycle repair class. Local bike clubs, YMCAs, or AYH Councils often offer inexpensive courses that are open to everyone. Or get hold of *Anybody's Bike Book* by Tom Cuthbertson (Ten Speed Press, 1971) from your local library or bookstore. This well-illustrated guide offers a no-nonsense approach to bicycle repair and maintenance.

Tool Kit. A good grasp of bicycle repair is of little use if you are stuck on a lonely road without the proper tools. Carry a small tool kit on your bicycle when you take a trip. Essentials include:

patch kit (for tire repair)	small screwdriver
pump (attached to bike)	pliers with wire-cutters
tire irons (for clincher tires)	cycle oil
adjustable crescent wrench (6 or 8 inch)	spoke wrench

Carry the following spare parts:

extra brake and gear cable	spare nuts and bolts
extra tube (or extra sew-ups)	extra brake blocks
spare spokes	

And for the more proficient repair artists:

vice grip	free-wheel remover
chain tool and spare links	allen wrenches

The accepted dress for the wheelman to-day is, in cool spring and autumn weather, a complete suit—coat, waistcoat, and knickerbockers—of serviceable gray or brown tweed, the coat cut very like an English pea-jacket, or what we prefer in America to call a "lounging coat." The waistcoat is high-buttoned; and the finish at the throat is a high roll-over linen collar and necktie of dull red or blue lustreless silk, with the alternative of a linen or pique stock tie. Colored linen seems more in keeping with the rough-and-ready cycling suit than white. Happily, the day has passed for the Scotch hose of vivid and eccentrically mixed colors and they are no longer admired and worn. Gray golf stockings, tastefully variegated with touches of black, white, and saber blue, or brown hose with very fine crisscrossing lines in yellow and red, now predominate. High or half-high laced shoes of black or brown leather dress the feet in good taste—that is, in harmony with the conservative preju-dices in dress so typical of the modern American man. Heavy gray or brown gloves and a small peaked cap made of the same goods as the suit, complete the costume.

From *Encyclopaedia of Etiquette:*
A Book of Manners for Everyday Use,
by Emily Holt (1901)

GEAR FOR A BICYCLE TOUR

The equipment you choose for your bicycle tour will depend upon the climate, the length of your trip, and your preferred type of accommodation. Generally, the longer your trip, the more gear you will need, such as extra clothing and, if you will not be near stores, extra food and fuel for your stove. If you camp out, you will need a sleeping bag and a tarp or tent. A lightweight cook stove may also be appropriate. Choosing instead to stay at hostels and budget motels will eliminate the extra weight and expense of camping equipment, but you will pay more for overnight accommodations (see *Low-Cost Accommodations* in Chapter 3).

Shoes. Sturdy sneakers with firm soles help distribute the power of your legs and feet evenly over the pedals. Energy is not lost in the constant flexing of the sole with each turn of the pedal, and cycling is more efficient. Although more expensive than sneakers, noncleated bicycle shoes protect your feet from injury, provide firm soles, and permit comfortable walking.

Raingear. A waterproof parka and chaps are one choice for cycling in the rain. Because a considerable amount of rain is tossed up from your wheels (unless you have fenders), rain capes and ponchos are not very effective. Ponchos in particular are useless and even dangerous in windy situations. One problem with waterproof parkas is that perspiration and body heat are also trapped inside the material, making cycling very uncomfortable. Gore Tex is a waterproof material that carries moisture away from your body through billions of microscopic pores. But with vigorous exercise moisture can still be temporarily trapped and body heat can become high. Gore Tex must also be kept clean, and is very expensive. Wool is a natural water-repellent material that is breathable, actually carries moisture away from your body to help keep you dry, and keeps you warm even when it's wet.

Bike Locks. Bicycle locks are appropriate for city riding and commuting, where your bike might be left unattended for a considerable amount of time. While there is no theft-proof locking system available today, a few precautions can be taken.

- Lock your bike to an immovable object such as a bicycle rack or telephone pole.
- Use a strong plastic-covered cable or heavy-gauge chain and a sturdy padlock. U-shaped locks made of stainless steel bar are available; they can lock your frame, rear wheel, and disconnected front wheel side by side to a small post. These locks weigh about 2½ pounds (see *Safety Equipment* in Chapter 3).
- Make sure that both front and rear wheel and frame are secured. You can disconnect the front wheel and lock it beside the rear wheel.
- Choose a public, lighted area to lock your bike.
- Keep the chain or cable high on the frame so bolt cutters can't be braced against the ground.

When touring in the countryside, locks may become cumbersome and are not always needed. Nevertheless, you can still take precautions against theft without using a lock.

- Wrap one or two bunji cords through your tires and leave your bike where you can see it if you're just going into a store or restaurant.
- If you're cycling with two or more people, leave one person behind to watch the bikes.

Front Bags. If you have ever fumbled through your saddlebags or struggled to take off a knapsack just to look at a map or take a quick picture, you can appreciate the convenience of a front handlebar bag. By just unzipping or flipping open the bag's top, you have: camera, map, hat, sunglasses, suntan lotion, a snack, a windbreaker, or bandana. Front bags also help distribute the weight of your load more evenly over your bicycle.

Saddlebags. For a long-distance bicycle tour, there is no replacement for good rear saddlebags. Hanging from both sides of your rear carrier, saddlebags distribute the weight of your load evenly over the rear wheel and keep a low center of gravity. A heavy pack carried on your back is not only uncomfortable, but unsafe: your center of gravity is too high, hampering your stability and control. Several styles and brands of saddlebags are available today. Look for bags made of durable, waterproof nylon. Compare systems for fastening the bags to your rear carrier. How securely do they attach? How easily can you remove them? How much room does each bag have? How easy it is to get into the bag to store and retrieve your gear? Compare features and prices, and buy only what you need.

Rear Carriers. Again, you have many choices. An aluminum alloy, rattrap-type of carrier is an inexpensive, dependable choice for touring. In any case, look for a sturdy carrier that has little side-to-side motion when mounted and loaded with gear.

Sleeping Bags. You can choose today from several durable models and styles of sleeping bags. Bags with goosedown fill provide the most warmth per ounce, and are also the most expensive. Because down depends on its loft, or its fluffed thickness, to provide its warmth, it becomes useless when wet. The down mats and the bag loses its warming capacity. Alternatives are found in synthetic fills—PolarGuard and Hollofil II. Although these bags are heavier and bulkier than down bags, they maintain their loft and warming capacity even when wet. Hollofil II, for instance, will absorb only 1 percent of available moisture. These bags dry fast and are generally less expensive than down. For comparison, 2 pounds 10 ounces of goosedown fill will keep the average person warm down to about −15°F., while 2 pounds 10 ounces of PolarGuard fill will keep that same person warm down to about 20°F. For maximum warmth, choose mummy bag construction, and use these bags with a closed cell ensolite pad.

Tents and Tarps. Unless you are expecting a lot of rain or a lot of mosquitoes, a tarp is quite adequate for bicycle camping. A tarp is easy to pitch, is inexpensive, and is considerably lighter than a tent. However, if rain or mosquitoes are a factor, by all means bring a tent. Tents come today in all shapes and sizes. You can, for instance, choose from a 6-pound, 2-person, I-pole tent; a 6½-pound, 2-person, A-frame tent; or a 5-pound, 10-ounce geodesic dome tent. Prices range from about $75 to well over $235. Look for light weight (you'll be carrying the tent around with you) and durable waterproof construction. The floor should be of waterproof nylon taffeta that extends a few inches up the walls. Doors should be zippered, easy to climb through, and have good mosquito netting. A separate rainfly of rip-stop nylon will help prevent condensation on the inside of the tent and shed heavy rain. Seams and joints should be double stitched, and poles should be of sturdy seamless aluminum.

Stoves. If you plan to do a lot of cooking on your trip, bring a small stove. Campfires are more romantic, but require more time and care. If it is raining, if you pull into camp late, or if campground rules prohibit, you may have to do without a campfire. Unless you like cold food, you will be happy you brought a stove. The most durable and dependable stoves are models that operate on Coleman fuel or white gas and have a small pump to pressurize them. These stoves require no priming and can be started with relative ease in cold weather. Stoves that run on butane or propane cartridges are lighter and less expensive, but are difficult to start in cold weather. Also, replacement cartridges may be hard to find on the road. Stoves that do require priming are generally durable and light-weight, but sometimes require care and patience when starting up. Make sure you read all operating instructions and keep your stove cleaned and properly maintained.

For manufacturers and mail order sources of bicycle gear, safety equipment, and camping gear, see *Equipment for You & Your Bike* in Chapter 3.

WEIGHT

Minimizing the weight you will carry on a bicycle tour requires restraint and imagination. For instance, one change of clothes is adequate; while you wear one set, wash the other set and hang it over the back of your bike to dry. Your bandana can serve as a hat, washcloth, and even dish towel. Do you need a whole mess kit? Why not eat right out of your frying pan instead of bringing along and dirtying up a plate. Will you use all the blades on your pocket knife, or will a simple utility knife do? Mail film and unneeded maps home after you've used them. Do you need a whole tube of toothpaste? While you're still planning your trip at home, set aside a partially used tube. And how about setting aside an almost used-up roll of toilet paper? After you've climbed a long hill or two, you're sure to think of some other ways to save weight.

GEAR FOR A ONE-DAY TRIP

Bicycle Equipment
- handlebar bag
- pump
- water bottle
- tool kit
- fanny bumper (see *Bicycle Safety* in Chapter 2)
- helmet*

Clothing
- windbreaker
- raingear*

*optional

Miscellaneous
- hat with brim
- cycling gloves
- sunglasses
- suntan lotion
- first aid kit
- extra food
- bike lock*
- camera and film*
- front light*
- maps

GEAR FOR AN EXTENDED TRIP

Bicycle Equipment
- saddlebags
- rear carrier
- pump
- water bottle(s)
- tool kit
- fanny bumper
- front light
- helmet*
- bike lock*
- 2–4 bunji cords
- handlebar bag*

Camping Gear
- tent or tarp
- sleeping bag
- ensolite pad

For Hostels
- sheet sleeping sack
- AYH or IYHF membership card

Cooking
- can opener
- stove*
- fuel bottle(s) and extra fuel*
- eating utensils
- mess kit
- pot scrubber

Personal
- 1–2 pair shorts
- 1 pair long pants
- 2 short sleeve shirts
- 1 long sleeve shirt
- 2–3 pair socks
- 2–3 pair underwear
- wool sweater
- nylon shell windbreaker
- raingear
- sneakers or cycling shoes
- towel and toilet articles

*optional

Miscellaneous

bandana
moneybag*
cycling gloves
hat with brim
sunglasses
suntan lotion
first aid kit

sewing kit*
insect repellent*
nylon cord
flashlight*
camera and film*
maps
extra food

*optional

HOW TO PACK

Packing a bicycle is truly an art. When all your gear is piled up, you may wonder if it will all fit on your bicycle. Well, sometimes it won't. Cut back; a seasoned cycle tourist can usually fit everything he or she needs in two saddlebags, in a front bag, and on top of a rear carrier. Here are a few suggestions:

- Pack so you can find things. Roll your clothes and pack them vertically in plastic bags. The bags help keep out moisture, keep your clothes organized, and allow you to pick out items at a glance from the top of your pack.
- Balance the weight on each side of your bicycle.
- Make sure the saddlebags are securely attached to your rear carrier. If your bags don't already have stiffeners, put stiff cardboard on the inside of each saddlebag so they won't sag into the spokes.
- Set saddlebags far enough back on your rear carrier so that your heels won't hit the bags while you pedal.
- Pack small items such as first aid kit, cup, hat, camera, and suntan lotion in the end pockets of your saddlebags or in your handlebar bag for quick and easy access.
- Strap your sleeping bag, ensolite pad, and tent (if you are carrying one) firmly over the top of the rear carrier with elastic bunji cords.

An organized bicycle tourist who spends only a little time each day packing and unpacking has more time to spend on important things—like relaxing, sight-seeing, and, of course, cycling.

CHAPTER TWO

On the Road

BICYCLE SAFETY

When you climb onto your bicycle and head out onto the road, remember one thing: cars and trucks are bigger than you are, so in a head-to-head confrontation get out of their way! With that simple thought in mind, we can proceed with our discussion.

A bicycle is generally considered a legal vehicle with a legitimate right to the road. But just how much right you have to the road differs from state to state. In some jurisdictions bicycles have the same rights and responsibilities as motor vehicles: they can occupy a full lane on many roads, they must signal when turning, and they must obey all traffic signs and traffic laws. In other jurisdictions bicycles can still use the road, but only the extreme right-hand portion of it. In still other areas a bicycle cannot use the road if there is an adjacent bicycle path. It is your responsibility to know the rules and regulations that govern bicycle use in the area you will travel through.

General Rules. The following general rules apply to bicycle use. Obey all traffic laws. Stop at stop signs, obey traffic lights, and always ride on the right with traffic. Do not ride the wrong way on a one-way street. Do not unnecessarily impede traffic. Signal when turning or when changing lanes. Never carry other people on your bike, or packages that will impede your control. Always watch out for cars and trucks; sometimes drivers simply don't see you.

Safety Devices. Wear brightly-colored clothing when you cycle. You will stand out from your background and motorists will see you much more readily. Orange triangles (or fanny bumpers) with reflective tape that tie around your waist and orange reflective vests are available. These two devices can be seen at a distance by oncoming vehicles (see *Safety Equipment* in Chapter 3). They not only improve your visibility by day, but stand out in rainy weather and at night.

When you consider the vulnerability of your head to injury in a bicycle accident, bicycle helmets make good sense. Models ranging in price from $25 to $40 are on the market today (see *Safety Equipment* in Chapter 3). Choose a model that fits snugly, has a strap system that holds it securely, is lightweight, and provides adequate ventilation on hot, sunny days. Hockey helmets are less costly, but they just don't absorb shock as well.

Tiny rearview mirrors that clip on your helmet or glasses are useful for keeping an eye on traffic coming up behind you (see *Safety Equipment* in Chapter 3). Bells are good for warning pedestrians on city streets and bicycle paths. Cycling gloves cushion your hands from road vibrations and protect your palms in case of a fall on gravel or pavement.

City Riding. Watch out for broken glass and potholes, and for loose debris along shoulders. Watch out for cars turning right just in front of you. Usually they don't see a cyclist coming up behind them, and often they fail to signal. Be especially cautious in jurisdictions where right-turn-on-red is permitted. Always be alert for opening doors on parked cars. If you see a person sitting in a parked car, make eye contact with him in his side-view mirror to be sure he sees you coming. Because a cyclist takes up so little space on city streets, drivers sometimes just don't see you. Cycle defensively and always wear bright clothing. Pedestrians are also a hazard. Watch for people walking out from between cars and for people leaving streetcorner curbs before the light changes.

Country Riding. Where poor shoulders prevail along roads, leave yourself some room from the edge of the pavement. If you start to slip down onto the shoulder, don't try to quickly jerk your front tire back onto the road. Just ride onto the shoulder, slow down, and climb back onto the road when you know the coast is clear. When cycling on dirt or gravel roads, ride slowly and steadily in a low (uphill) gear.

When cycling with a group on a busy road, ride in single file. If you want to pass someone, check behind you for approaching traffic (a rearview mirror is helpful here), and then alert the cyclist ahead of you that you're passing. Also alert other cyclists when cars are approaching from the rear. When riding two abreast, the rider nearest the center of the road drops back for approaching traffic. Always cross railroad tracks at a right angle, and avoid storm sewer gratings.

Before long downhills, check your brakes. If it's cool, put on an extra layer of clothing. Tighten down your hat. Once you start down, don't look back. Pump your brakes to slow down—applying both brakes continually can cause your rims to overheat and risk a tire blowout. Pedal from time to time to keep your legs warm and loose. Keep both hands on the dropped portion of the handlebars at all times for proper body position and for quick braking if needed. Watch the road ahead for loose gravel, chuckholes, water, or other hazards. Slow down before going into a curve and lean as you turn. Keep your mouth closed—bugs traveling at high speeds leave an unpleasant taste.

Dogs are a special challenge. If you have any doubts about your ability to outrun, outsmart, or drive off a pursuing dog, stop, get off your bike, and keep the bike between you and the dog. If you slowly walk away from the dog's front yard he will usually lose interest in you. Running into or over a dog in an effort to outrun him can result in serious injury—both to you and to the dog!

Bad Weather. When riding in the rain, keep in mind that it takes about twice as long for your rim brakes to grip. Also, your rubber tires will skid much more easily, especially when turning. During periods of fog, road visibility is greatly reduced. Use a front light and reflective vest or fanny bumper. Strong side winds and head winds present a serious physical challenge and limit your ability to hear upcoming traffic. Such a situation requires slow, steady riding and alert reactions to quick gusts of wind.

Night Riding. Avoid night riding whenever possible. If you commute and must ride at night, invest in a good front and rear light, wear a helmet, and wear a reflective vest. If you are in the country and it's an emergency, use a front light, make sure you have a rear reflector, wear a reflective vest or fanny bumper, and cycle defensively.

- Clamp each brake, making sure the pads grip the rims firmly and squarely. As you clamp each brake, try to push the bike forward. The respective wheels should not turn.
- Grab the unloaded bicycle and bounce it gently, checking for any loose parts or rattles.
- Check each wheel for any side play in the hub.
- Make sure each tire is properly inflated.
- Grab the front wheel between your knees from the front of the bike and make sure the handlebars are tight.
- Load your bike carefully and make sure all items are securely attached and the weight properly balanced.

GETTING IN SHAPE

Being in good physical shape for a bicycle trip will enhance your riding comfort, reduce the risk of injury or accident due to fatigue, and improve your on-the-road attitude. Before you begin a rigorous exercise program, get a thorough medical checkup. This is especially important if you're over thirty or have a history of cardiovascular disease or other health difficulties.

Begin gradually. Ride your bike at least three or four times a week, slowly increasing the distance you travel and then the weight you carry. You can combine this conditioning with trips to work or a day-long ride to a nearby park. You can also supplement your conditioning with other forms of exercise, such as swimming, jogging, or tennis.

Ride your bike for periods of about one hour, followed by a rest period of up to ten minutes. Walk around to relax your muscles and to help keep them from tightening up. Don't stop just after a hard climb. Keep riding, or walk your bike for a few minutes to keep your legs loose.

A good diet is an important part of your conditioning program. Eat a balanced meal about two hours before you start exercising. Carbohydrates are more useful than fats. Bring along some extra food when cycling. Peanut butter is a good source of protein and carbohydrates. Bananas contain carbohydrates and help replace the potassium which your body loses through sweating. Bring along some water and take sips periodically to prevent dehydration. Avoid carbonated beverages—water and fruit juices are best. Also, avoid riding in extremely hot weather. Morning cycling is best.

Riding Technique. The manner in which you ride your bicycle will affect your endurance on a trip. Plan to ride about one mile in six minutes, or about 10 miles per hour. Cadence, or the rate at which you pedal, is of primary importance. Pedaling too fast in too low a gear can be tiring and can put a strain on your knees. Pedaling too slow in too high a gear results in a laborious, grinding cadence which will cause your body and bicycle to wobble and sway. Work yourself into a cadence which is comfortable and efficient for you. Generally, 65 to 80 pedal revolutions per minute is a good target. On long uphills, maintain brisk cadence by switching to lower gears. Don't try to grind your way to the top. Long climbs take time and patience.

Ankling permits you to distribute your strength evenly over the whole pedal revolution. Place the ball of your foot on the pedal (toe clips are extremely helpful here) and make an effort to point your toe down at the bottom of the revolution, and then to lift the pedal up. Ankling further increases riding efficiency.

Knee trouble can be a problem. When riding, knees should be parallel to the frame. Pointing them out increases stress on them. Cycling at too fast a cadence or letting your knees become chilled may cause them to give out. Keep your knees and other joints warm and dry, even if it means changing clothes.

Finally, don't underestimate the sun. Protect your head with a hat and use suntan lotion or sunscreen to block out ultraviolet rays. Road glare, dry wind, and high altitudes combine to increase the intensity of the sun on your skin.

TRANSPORTING YOUR BIKE

By Car. You can choose between two types of commercially built bicycle carriers for your car. Carriers that fit on the back bumper of your car are the least expensive. Look for models with teflon or rubber-coated hanger hooks with two dips into which you can fit two bicycles. The metal parts of the carrier should be covered with a soft plastic coating to prevent scratching of your bike. Generally, bumper carriers will accommodate no more than two bicycles. Your bicycles should not extend beyond the sides of your car, and should not block your tail lights.

Roof racks can generally accommodate up to six bicycles. Make sure the rack is securely fastened to the car and that each bike is firmly in place before you start. Detach loose items such as bicycle pumps and front bags. You may also, of course, choose to build your own bicycle rack, using these commercial models as examples.

By Bus. Bicycles must be broken down and placed in a cardboard carton. Remove the bike's front wheel and tie it to the frame. Turn the handlebars sideways. Turn one or both pedals inward. Once placed in a tight-fitting carton, secure and protect the bike with crumpled newspapers. Tie the box shut with rope or cord. Your bike can be shipped in advance of your departure, when you leave, or at a later date. Bus companies don't assess any excess baggage charge, and they don't supply boxes. Cartons are usually obtained from a local bicycle shop.

By Train. All bicycles accepted as checked baggage or express baggage by AMTRAK must be enclosed in a carton. You may provide your own carton, or purchase cartons for $4 at any station eligible to accept bicycles for shipment. Three pieces of baggage are allowed as a ticketed passenger, and the boxed bicycle is counted as one piece of checked baggage. Check with your AMTRAK agent for trains and stations that accept bicycles for shipment.

By Plane. On most flights within the United States and Hawaii, there is a $12 charge for taking along a bicycle. Bikes must be boxed with pedals removed and the handlebars turned sideways. Some airlines have boxes available at the airport, so check with your specific carrier ahead of time.

Renting a Bike. You may choose to avoid the expense of buying a new bicycle or of transporting your own bicycle over a long distance by renting a bike. Many bicycle shops and outfitters around the country rent bicycles by the hour or by the day. Expect to pay about $10 a day in the city and up to $8 a day in the country. Ten-speed bikes are generally more expensive to rent than one- and three-speeds.

A BICYCLE TOURING MENU

A cyclist pedals on his or her stomach. If you are eating well, most likely you are performing well and enjoying your trip to its fullest. The key to good eating is to plan ahead. Have you brought along enough money to buy your food? Do you know where the next store is along your route? Did you bring along a cook stove and mess kit to prepare hot meals? If you have a handle on these considerations your trip should go very well.

Budget. The money you spend on food will vary with the size of the store and the items purchased. Plan to spend anywhere from $4 to $5 per day for food. A group of cyclists can expect to pay a little less per person. Shop wisely. Compare prices between different brands of the same item. Look for the price per ounce on canned, boxed, frozen, or prepackaged items. You can save money by buying certain items in bulk and then carrying them with you: peanut butter, noodles, rice, cheese, honey, etc. Buy fruits and vegetables in season. Check the price per pound on meat, poultry, cheese, etc., and be prepared to alter your menu if certain items are priced too high. Finally, avoid restaurants except for an occasional treat or emergency. They will ruin your daily budget.

Buying Food. Plan a balanced diet. Every day's menu should include something from each of the following food groups:

- Meats, poultry, or fish—dried peas or beans can be substituted on occasion for variety.
- Vegetables—one or more servings of a green, leafy, or yellow vegetable; other vegetables in season, some raw, some cooked; potatoes.
- Cereals and bread—granola, enriched cereals, whole grain breads.
- Fruits—one or more servings of oranges, grapefruit, tomatoes, or raw cabbage.
- Dairy products—eggs, cheese, milk, and yogurt for calcium and protein.
- Fats—butter, margarine, nuts, peanut butter.
- Other—sweets and desserts occasionally for a treat or for quick energy.

Vegetarians whose daily diet includes an egg, two cups of milk, a cup of yogurt, and two ounces of cheese will get all the protein, calcium, and riboflavin they need as well as 50 percent of their vitamin A and 25 percent of their thiamine requirement. By adding fruits, vegetables, some whole grain bread, and enriched cereal vegetarians will get generous amounts of most of the nutrients they need. Vegetarians should use iodized salt and vitamin D fortified milk to complete their nutritional requirements.

Don't overlook fruit and vegetable stands you may pass along the road. The produce is fresh and the prices are generally lower than in a supermarket. Mixing fresh strawberries, blueberries, and apple or peach slices with cottage cheese or yogurt can be a lunch in itself. Be sure you wash all fruits and vegetables before you eat them.

Prepackaged freeze-dried foods are sometimes appropriate if you will not be coming across stores or towns on your trip. Price per serving for these foods is extremely high, however, and serving portions listed on the label are usually inadequate for a cyclist's healthy appetite. Basic staples such as noodles, rice, peanut butter, honey, etc., should still comprise the bulk of your diet. Cheese, margarine, oranges, apples, and potatoes also keep well if packed properly and kept out of the sun.

Proportions. Buy your food according to the following proportions:

- Meat—¼ lb. per person if it will be combined in a one-pot meal. Allow ⅓ lb. per person otherwise.
- Fish or poultry—½ lb. per person.
- Vegetables—⅓ lb. of fresh vegetables, 4 oz. of canned vegetables, 4 oz. of frozen vegetables per person minimum.
- Rice—1 to 1½ cups of cooked rice per person. Uncooked rice: 1 cup = 3 cups cooked. Precooked (Minute) rice: 1 cup = 2 cups cooked.
- Spaghetti or macaroni—1 to 1½ cups of cooked spaghetti or macaroni per person. 1 lb. of either equals 8 cups cooked.
- Milk—one quart has four 8-oz cups.

Don't overlook spices. Salt, pepper, oregano, garlic, onions, chili powder, cinnamon, etc., are all welcome and tasty additions to any meal.

Carrying Food. Store fresh foods in durable airtight Ziploc bags. Perishable foods should be packed out of the sun in your saddlebags. To save weight, transfer such items as peanut butter, jelly, and honey from jars into plastic squeeze tubes. These squeeze tubes look like toothpaste tubes and are available at camping and sporting goods stores. Cereal boxes, crackers, spaghetti, cookies, etc., can be strapped temporarily under elastic bunji cords over the top of your gear. Squashable items such as bread can be tied from the end of the plastic wrapper to a bunji cord and left to flop around.

Fruits, cans, glass jars, and other items that might slip out from under a bunji cord should be packed inside your saddlebags. Or pack them in a mesh onion bag and tie the bag over your gear. Pack egg cartons carefully on top of or between clothes in your saddlebags.

Menu Suggestions. The following foods are especially appropriate on a bicycle tour:

- Peanut butter—it tastes good, is a good source of protein, provides energy, fills you up, and isn't very expensive. Combine it with honey, jelly, or just eat it with your finger.
- Gorp—short for "good ole raisins and peanuts." To make gorp, mix appropriate amounts of salted peanuts, raisins, M&M's, and, if you desire, cashews, walnuts, dates, coconut, etc. Gorp is an excellent high energy snack food for any time of the day. Pack gorp in durable Ziploc bags.
- Lemonade—most convenient in dried form. The sugar provides quick energy, the lemonade provides vitamin C, and it tastes a lot better than plain water.
- Bananas—they supply carbohydrates and replace the potassium your body loses through sweating. Pack them carefully.
- Instant soup—it's quick, warm, and delicious after a long day on the road. It also helps replace the salt your body loses through sweating.
- Macaroni & cheese—simple, filling, and tasty. Provides protein and carbohydrates. Use fresh cheese if possible. Add ham or hot dogs for variety.
- S'Mores—for a special treat. Roasted marshmallows and squares of chocolate bars between two graham crackers. Great with milk or tea, and for nostalgic girl scouts.

On a bicycle trip, dinner should be your big meal. Keep breakfast simple. Hot or cold cereal, fruit, fruit juice, milk, and hot drinks are good. You may occasionally want to cook up eggs, pancakes, or French toast, but set aside more time on such mornings. Eat lunch on the road, or spread lunch out into several daily snacks, using peanut butter, gorp, cheese, yogurt, or fresh fruit. Cook up a good hot dinner as often as you can. You should spend about half of your daily food budget on dinner.

Clean-Up. Soak dishes containing milk, eggs, hot cereal, and starches in cold water. Hot water cooks these food particles harder. Use hot water to clean dishes containing fat or grease. Use a pot scrubber to clean tough jobs. Baking soda mixed with water (three tablespoons to one quart of water) also works well on tough jobs. When cooking over an open fire, apply a liquid soap beforehand to the outsides of pots and pans. This makes cleaning much easier. On the other hand, pots and pans with blackened bottoms will heat up faster. Just be sure to pack them away in durable plastic bags before returning them to your saddlebags. Don't leave a messy campsite; pack out all your trash.

Pests. Protect your food at night from small pests. Porcupines, chipmunks, raccoons, and mice can be both annoying and destructive. Wrap food in odorproof plastic bags. Hang food in a strong garbage bag or stuff sack from a sturdy tree limb. In bear country, make sure your food sack is hung away from camp on a tree limb at least eight feet off the ground and four feet out from the tree's trunk. Do not keep food near your tent or sleeping bag!

LEADING A GROUP

No one can teach you to be a leader. Clear thinking and good judgment are qualities acquired through experience. But if you have leadership abilities to begin with, certain knowledge will enhance those talents.

Generally, one leader should take on no more than ten individuals. A group of eight is more functional, while twelve is unwieldy for one leader. In the latter case, another leader or an assistant leader is appropriate. Groups of more than twelve can be distracting to motorists and create logistical problems at stores, campgrounds, and hostels. Keep your group small, even if it means splitting up.

A leader is responsible for the safety and well-being of his or her group. Research your trip carefully, using good road maps, current campground directories, your AYH Hostel Handbook, and other relevant literature. Make some local contacts in advance to secure personal and up-to-date information. Be in good shape: you must set a good example for the rest of your group. Know bike repair well and bring along a good selection of tools and parts. You most certainly will be called upon sooner or later to help fix a group member's bike. Know your first aid and bring along a complete group first aid kit. Your best bet is to take a first aid course taught by your local American Red Cross chapter.

Emphasize the importance and urgency of safety. If you are leading first-time bike tourers, you may find that many of them have never bicycled beyond their neighborhood streets. Point out the hazards of traffic on busy roads, and don't put up with unsafe riding habits.

Daily Dynamics. Get your group up at a reasonable hour. The morning hours are often your best cycling hours, providing cooler temperatures and lighter traffic. If you have one or more group members who are slow to get organized in the morning, get them up earlier, or have them pack the night before.

After breakfast, have everyone perform the *Cyclist's Quick Check* on their own bike (see Chapter 2). Then give everyone the address and phone number of that evening's overnight stop. That way anyone who gets lost can still get in touch with you. If group members don't have their own maps, give them written directions for the day's route. Also, designate a place to meet for lunch. Appoint an assistant leader to ride up front if you like. You may have a particular person in mind, or switch from day to day. As leader, it's your job to bring up the rear. That way you'll catch up to any technical or medical problems that might arise, rather than ride away from them.

If a group member rides very slowly, be patient. Check his bike—there may be a mechanical problem. Maybe he needs to send extra weight home. Maybe his riding technique is bad. Or maybe he's just plain slow. Give him a head start.

Usually the group will get pretty well spread out in the course of the day. You'll always have your fast riders and your slow riders.

One method to keep people from getting lost and getting too far apart is to use the "peel-off" system. Example: rider #1 comes to an intersection, stops, and waits. Rider #2 arrives, and rider #1 leaves. Rider #2 then waits for rider #3 before leaving, and so on. This way everyone proceeds in the same direction as the last person. If they have gone the wrong way, at least they've all gone the wrong way together, and you know where they are.

Stress good conduct to all your group members. As part of a group, they not only represent themselves, but represent and reflect upon the whole group. If your group is part of an organization that will send other groups to the same area, good conduct is especially important. You will want future groups to be received in the same friendly manner that you were.

Feeding a Group. A well-fed group is a happy group. Don't let group members go hungry. If you have vegetarians in your group, try to compromise. Fix meals in which meats can be separated out, and plan a vegetarian meal or two for the whole group.

Divide your group up and assign chores. Have a shopping detail, a cooking detail, and a clean-up detail (or suitable arrangement of your own choosing). Rotate the assignments so everyone has a chance to do a little of each. When buying food, don't send everyone into the store at once. Arguments will likely ensue over what to buy and how much to buy (six for Fig Newtons to four for Oreos!). Leave buying to the shopping detail, offering your advice and assistance when needed. Using this system encourages group members to be more responsible and more involved. It also removes the burden from your own shoulders. And dinner will always be an adventure!

Liability. As leader, the responsibility for the safety of your group rests squarely upon your shoulders. If you are leading for an organization, make sure they have a comprehensive liability policy that covers your activities as leader.

Liability is based on the principle of negligence. Negligence is the failure to act as a reasonably prudent person would act under the circumstance. It is conduct which falls below the standard established by law for the protection of others against unreasonable risks. Anticipation is the key. If you are aware of hazards and make a reasonable effort to avoid them, liability is minimized.

CHAPTER THREE
Sources of Information

STATE HIGHWAY MAPS, TRAVEL INFORMATION & COUNTY ROAD MAPS

The bicycle route maps in *The American Bicycle Atlas* have been researched and drawn with a great deal of care. Nevertheless, you may want to supplement these bicycle route maps with road maps and travel literature distributed by individual states. These road maps and information packages are particularly useful if you should leave the suggested bicycle routes and do some exploring on your own.

State highway maps are published for free distribution by all forty-eight continental states. Alaska, Hawaii, and the District of Columbia are exceptions. These maps generally show main roadways and public campgrounds. However, little secondary road detail is given. All fifty states and the District of Columbia have travel information offices which distribute free tourist information on request. Usually this information includes a state highway map.

County road maps are published by most states. These maps are generally drawn to a scale of 1″ = 1 mile, ½″ = 1 mile, or ¼″ = 1 mile. Secondary road detail is excellent, but on longer tours you will need to carry a large number of these maps. Individual counties may comprise from one to several map sheets, and prices per sheet range from free to about $2.50. Some states charge for sales tax and postage. Write for free indexes.

STATE HIGHWAY MAPS & COUNTY ROAD MAPS

Alabama
Alabama Bureau of Publicity &
    Information
532 South Perry St.
Montgomery, AL 36130

*State of Alabama Highway
    Dept.
Bureau of State Planning
Montgomery, AL 36130

Alaska
Alaska State Division of
    Tourism
Pouch E
Juneau, AK 99811

Arizona
Arizona Dept. of
    Transportation
206 South 17th Ave.
Phoenix, AZ 85007

Arizona State Office of Tourism
1700 West Washington, Rm.
    500
Phoenix, AZ 85007

*Arizona Dept. of
    Transportation
Mail Drop 134A
206 South 17th Ave.
Phoenix, AZ 85007

Arkansas
*Arkansas State Hwy. &
    Transportation Dept.
Map Sales—Rm. 204
P.O. Box 2261
Little Rock, AR 72203

Arkansas Division of Tourism
Dept. of Parks & Tourism
149 State Capitol Bldg.
Little Rock, AR 72201

Arkansas State Hwy. &
    Transportation Dept.
Map Sales—Rm. 204
P.O. Box 2261
Little Rock, AR 72203

California
Office of Visitor Services
California Dept. of Economic
    & Business Development
P.O. Box 1499
Sacramento, CA 95805

*Caltrans
Office Engineer
Cartographic Services
P.O. Box 1499
Sacramento, CA 95807

Colorado
Colorado Division of Highways
4201 East Arkansas Ave.
Denver, CO 80222

Colorado Office of Tourism
500 State Centennial Bldg.
1313 Sherman St.
Denver, CO 80203

*Colorado Division of Highways
Administrative Services
4201 E. Arkansas Ave., Rm.
    117
Denver, CO 80222

County road map.

29

Connecticut
Connecticut Dept. of
     Transportation
24 Wolcott Hill Rd.
Wethersfield, CT 06109

Tourism Division
Conn. Dept. of Economic
     Development
210 Washington St.
Hartford, CT 06106

*Conn. Dept. of Transportation
24 Wolcott Hill Rd.
Wethersfield, CT 06109

Delaware
Delaware Dept. of
     Transportation
P.O. Box 778
Dover, DE 19901

Delaware State Travel Service
630 State College Rd.
P.O. Box 1401
Dover, DE 19901

*Delaware Dept. of
     Transportation
P.O. Box 778
Dover, DE 19901
Attn: Administrative Manager

District of Columbia
Metropolitan Washington
     Council of Governments
     (COG)
1225 Connecticut Ave., NW
Washington, DC 20036
(*Bicycle Paths in the
     Washington Area*, $2)

Washington Convention &
     Visitors Association
1575 "I" St., NW, Suite 250
Washington, DC 20005

Florida
Florida Division of Tourism
107 W. Gaines St., Rm. 505
Tallahassee, FL 32301

*Florida Dept. of
     Transportation
Maps & Publications Section
Mail Station 12, Rm. 27
605 Suwannee St.
Tallahassee, FL 32301

Georgia
Georgia Dept. of
     Transporation
No. 2 Capitol Square
Atlanta, GA 30334

Georgia Tourist Division
Dept. of Industry & Trade
P.O. Box 1776
Atlanta, GA 30301

*Georgia Dept. of
     Transportation
Map Sales—Rm. 10
No. 2 Capitol Square
Atlanta, GA 30334

Hawaii
State Highway Division
Planning Branch
Drafting & Mapping Section
600 Kapiolani Blvd., Suite 310
Honolulu, HI 96814
(individual maps of islands)

Hawaii Visitors Bureau
2270 Kalakaua Ave., Suite 801
Honolulu, HI 96815

Idaho
*Idaho Transportation Dept.
P.O. Box 7129
Boise, ID 83707

Idaho Division of Tourism &
    Industrial Development
State Capitol Bldg., Rm. 108
Boise, ID 83720

Idaho Transportation Dept.
P.O. Box 7129
Boise, ID 83707

Illinois
Illinois Dept. of Transportation
2300 S. Dirksen Pkwy.
Springfield, IL 62764

Illinois Office of Tourism
222 South College St.
Springfield, IL 62707

*Map Sales
217 Administration Bldg.
Illinois Dept. of Transportation
2300 S. Dirksen Pkwy.
Springfield, IL 62764

Indiana
Indiana State Hwy.
    Commission
100 North Senate Av.
Indianapolis, IN 46204

Indiana Tourism Development
    Division
Dept. of Commerce

440 North Meridian St.
Indianapolis, IN 46204

*The Marbaugh Engineering
    Supply Co.
4145 North Keystone Av.
Indianapolis, IN 46205

Iowa
Iowa Dept. of Transportation
826 Lincoln Way
Ames, IA 50010

Travel Division
Iowa Development
    Commission
250 Jewett Bldg.
Des Moines, IA 50309

*Iowa Dept. of Transportation
826 Lincoln Way
Ames, IA 50010

Kansas
Kansas Dept. of Transportation
State Office Bldg.
Topeka, KS 66612

Kansas Dept. of Economic
    Development
503 Kansas Ave., 6th Floor
Topeka, KS 66603

*Planning & Development
    Dept.
Kansas Dept. of Transportation
State Office Bldg., 8th Floor
Topeka, KS 66612

Kentucky
Kentucky Dept. of
    Transportation

County road map.

31

Office of Transportation
    Planning
Division of Facilities Planning
419 Ann St.
Frankfort, KY 40622

Kentucky Dept. of Tourism
Fort Boone Plaza
Frankfort, KY 40601

*Kentucky Dept. of
    Transportation
Map Sales
419 Ann St.
Frankfort, KY 40622

Louisiana
Louisiana Dept. of
    Transportation &
    Development
Office of Highways
Baton Rouge, LA 70804

Louisiana Office of Tourism
P.O. Box 44291, Capitol
    Station
Baton Rouge, LA 70804

*Louisiana Dept. of
    Transportation &
    Development
General Files Unit
P.O. Box 44245, Capitol
    Station
Baton Rouge, LA 70804

Maine
Maine Dept. of Transportation
Special Services Division
Transportation Bldg.
Augusta, ME 04333

The Maine Publicity Bureau
97 Winthrop St.
Hollowell, ME 04347

*Maine Dept. of Transportation
Special Services Division
Transportation Bldg.
Augusta, ME 04333

Maryland
Maryland Dept. of
    Transportation
State Hwy. Administration
Baltimore, MD 21201

Maryland Office of Tourism
    Development
1748 Forest Dr.
Annapolis, MD 21401

*State Hwy. Administration
Map Distribution Section
2323 West Joppa Rd.
Brooklandville, MD 21022

Massachusetts
Bureau of Transportation
    Planning & Development
Mass. Dept. of Public Works
150 Causeway St., Rm. 301
Boston, MA 02114

Bureau of Vacation Travel
100 Cambridge St.
Boston, MA 02202

*Bureau of Transportation
    Planning & Development
Mass. Dept. of Public Works
150 Causeway St., Rm. 301
Boston, MA 02114

Michigan
Michigan Dept. of
Transportation
P.O. Box 30050
Lansing, MI 48909

Travel Bureau
Michigan Dept. of Commerce
P.O. Box 30226
Lansing, MI 48909

*Dept. of State Highways &
Transportation
Bike Maps
P.O. Box 30050
Lansing, MI 48909
(free county by county bike
maps)

Minnesota
Minnesota Dept. of
Transportation
John Ireland Blvd.
St. Paul, MN 55155

Minnesota Tourism Bureau
480 Cedar St.
St. Paul, MN 55101

*Minnesota Dept. of
Transportation
John Ireland Blvd.
Room B-20
St. Paul, MN 55155

Mississippi
Mississippi State Hwy. Dept.
P.O. Box 1850
Jackson, MS 39205

Mississippi Division of
Tourism

Dept. of Economic
Development
P.O. Box 849
Jackson, MS 39205

*Mississippi State Hwy. Dept.
Map Sales
P.O. Box 1850
Jackson, MS 39205

Missouri
Missouri Hwy. &
Transportation Dept.
P.O. Box 270
Jefferson City, MO 65102

Missouri Division of Tourism
308 East High St.
Jefferson City, MO 65101

*Missouri Hwy. &
Transportation Dept.
P.O. Box 270
Jefferson City, MO 65102

Montana
Montana Dept. of Highways
Travel Promotion Unit
Helena, MT 59601

*Montana Dept. of Highways
Planning & Research Bureau
Helena, MT 59601

Nebraska
Nebraska Dept. of Roads
Information Office
P.O. Box 94759
Lincoln, NE 68509

Nebraska Dept. of Economic
Development

County road map.

33

Travel & Tourism Division
P.O. Box 94666
Lincoln, NE 68509

*Nebraska Dept. of Roads
Information Office
P.O. Box 94759
Lincoln, NE 68509

Nevada
Nevada State Hwy. Dept.
Public Information Office
1263 South Stewart St.
Carson City, NV 89712

Nevada Dept. of Economic
Development
Division of Tourism
Capitol Complex
1050 East Williams
Carson City, NV 89710

*Nevada State Hwy. Dept.
Map Section—Rm. 206
1263 South Stewart St.
Carson City, NV 89712

New Hampshire
Planning & Economics
Division
Dept. of Public Works &
Hwys.
John O. Morton State Office
Bldg.
Concord, NH 03301

New Hampshire Office of
Vacation Travel
Dept. of Resources &
Economic Development
P.O. Box 856
6 Loudon Rd.
Concord, NH 03301

*Planning & Economics
Division
Dept. of Public Works &
Hwys.
John O. Morton State Office
Bldg.
Concord, NH 03301

New Jersey
New Jersey Dept. of
Transportation
1035 Parkway Ave.
P.O. Box 101
Trenton, NJ 08625

New Jersey Division of Travel
& Tourism
Dept. of Labor & Industry
P.O. Box 400
Trenton, NJ 08625

*New Jersey Dept. of
Transportation
Bureau of Data Resources
1035 Parkway Ave.
Trenton, NJ 08625

New Mexico
New Mexico State Hwy. Dept.
P.O. Box 1149
Room B-4
Santa Fe, NM 87503

Tourism & Travel Division
New Mexico Commerce &
Industry Dept.
Bataan Memorial Bldg.
Santa Fe, NM 87503

*New Mexico State Hwy. Dept.
P.O. Box 1149
Room B-4
Santa Fe, NM 87503

New York
New York State Dept. of
 Transportation
1220 Washington Ave.
State Campus
Albany, NY 12232

New York State Division of
 Tourism
Dept. of Commerce
230 Park Ave., Suite 866
New York, NY 10017

*New York State Dept. of
 Transportation
1220 Washington Ave.
State Campus
Albany, NY 12232

North Carolina
North Carolina Dept. of
 Transportation
Raleigh, NC 27611

North Carolina Division of
 Travel & Tourism
430 North Salisbury St.
Raleigh, NC 27611

*North Carolina Dept. of
 Transportation
Head of Location & Survey
 Unit
Division of Highways
Raleigh, NC 27611

North Dakota
North Dakota State Hwy.
 Dept.
Travel Division
Capitol Grounds
Bismarck, ND 58505

*North Dakota State Hwy.
 Dept.
Map Sales
Capitol Grounds
Bismarck, ND 58505

Ohio
Bureau of Public Information
25 South Front St.
Columbus, OH 43216

Ohio Office of Travel &
 Tourism
P.O. Box 1001
Columbus, OH 43216

*Ohio Dept. of Transportation
25 South Front St.
Room B100, P.O. Box 899
Columbus, OH 43216

Oklahoma
Oklahoma Dept. of
 Transportation
200 N.E. 21st St.
Oklahoma City, OK 73105

Division of Tourism Promotion
Oklahoma Tourism &
 Recreation Dept.
500 Will Rogers Bldg.
Oklahoma City, OK 73105

*Oklahoma Dept. of
 Transportation
Reproduction Branch
200 N.E. 21st St.
Oklahoma City, OK 73105

Oregon
Oregon Dept. of
 Transportation
Travel Information Section

County road map.

Transportation Bldg., Rm. 101
Salem, OR 97310

*Oregon Dept. of
    Transportation
Map Distribution Unit
Transportation Bldg., Rm. 17
Salem, OR 97310

Pennsylvania
Pennsylvania Dept. of
    Transportation
Bureau of Public Affairs
Harrisburg, PA 17120

Pennsylvania Bureau of Travel
    Development
Dept. of Commerce
206 South Office Bldg.
Harrisburg, PA 17120

*PennDOT Publication Sales
    Store
P.O. Box 134, Bldg. 33, HIA
Middletown, PA 17057

Rhode Island
Dept. of Economic
    Development
Tourist & Promotion Division
One Waybosset Hill
Providence, RI 02903

South Carolina
South Carolina Dept. of Hwys.
    & Public Transportation
P.O. Box 191
Columbia, SC 29202

South Carolina Dept. of Parks,
    Recreation & Tourism

Edgar A. Brown Bldg., Suite
    113
1205 Pendleton St.
Columbia, SC 29201

*South Carolina Dept. of Hwys.
    & Public Transportation
Map Sales, Traffic & Planning
    Section
P.O. Box 191
Columbia, SC 29202

South Dakota
South Dakota Division of
    Tourism
Joe Foss Bldg., Rm. 217
Pierre, SD 57501

*South Dakota Dept. of
    Transportation
Mapping Center
Transportation Bldg.
Pierre, SD 57501

Tennessee
Tennessee Dept. of
    Transportation
400 Doctors' Bldg.
706 Church St.
Nashville, TN 37203

Tennessee Dept. of Tourist
    Development
505 Fesslers Lane
Nashville, TN 37210

*Tennessee Dept. of
    Transportation
Office of Research & Planning
400 Doctors' Bldg.
706 Church St.
Nashville, TN 37203

Texas
State Dept. of Hwys. & Public
    Transportation
Travel & Information Division
P.O. Box 5064
Austin, TX 78763

Texas Tourist Development
    Agency
P.O. Box 12008, Capitol
    Station
Austin, TX 78711

*State Dept. of Hwys. & Public
    Transportation
Attn.: File D-10
P.O. Box 5051, W. Austin
    Station
Austin, TX 78763

Utah
Utah Dept. of Transportation
Suite 800
405 South Main St.
Salt Lake City, UT 84111

Utah Travel Council
Council Hall—Capitol Hill
Salt Lake City, UT 84114

Vermont
Agency of Development &
    Community Affairs
Vermont Travel Division
61 Elm St.
Montpelier, VT 05602

*Vermont Agency of
    Transportation
Planning Division—Mapping
    Section
Montpelier, VT 05602

Virginia
Virginia Dept. of Hwys. &
    Transportation
1221 East Broad St.
Richmond, VA 23219

Virginia State Travel Service
6 North Sixth St.
Richmond, VA 23219

*Virginia Dept. of Hwys. &
    Transportation
Office of Public Relations
1221 East Broad St.
Richmond, VA 23219

Washington
Washington Dept. of
    Transportation
Hwy. Administration Bldg.
Olympia, WA 98504

Washington Travel
    Development Division
Dept. of Commerce &
    Economic Development
312 First Ave., North
Seattle, WA 98109

*Washington Dept. of
    Transportation
Public Transportation &
    Planning
Hwy. Administration Bldg.
Olympia, WA 98504

West Virginia
West Virginia Dept. of Hwys.
1900 Washington St., East
Charleston, WV 25305

*County road map.

37

West Virginia Travel
    Development Division
Office of Economic &
    Community Development
1900 Washington St., East
Charleston, WV 25305

*West Virginia Dept. of Hwys.
Statewide Planning Division
1900 Washington St., East
Charleston, WV 25305

Wisconsin
Wisconsin Dept. of
    Transportation
4802 Sheboygan Ave.
Madison, WI 53702

Wisconsin Division of Tourism
Dept. of Business
    Development

123 W. Washington Ave., Rm.
    650
Madison, WI 53702

*Wisconsin Dept. of
    Transportation
Document Sales
P.O. Box 7426
Madison, WI 53707

Wyoming
Wyoming Highway Dept.
P.O. Box 1708
Cheyenne, WY 82001

Wyoming Travel Commission
Frank Norris, Jr., Travel
    Center
Cheyenne, WY 82002

*Wyoming Highway Dept.
P.O. Box 1708
Cheyenne, WY 82001

TRAIL GUIDES FOR THE TOURING BICYCLIST

With the inauguration in 1976 of the 4,250-mile Trans-America Bicycle Trail, a new era was begun in the development of long-distance touring routes nationwide. The many trails that exist today take advantage of a vast network of country roads and rural highways that crisscross our nation. They invite touring cyclists everywhere to linger for just a little while longer in America's great backyard. These routes have not been included among the several regional tours in *The American Bicycle Atlas*.

A list of trail guides appears below by region. Each trail guide describes a long-distance bicycle route which has been developed and mapped by one of several organizations or states. These bicycle routes make use of existing secondary roads, and take anywhere from a few days to several weeks to travel. Those trail guides described as "strip maps" are generally 4″ × 8″ map booklets which fit snugly on top of a front handlebar bag. Costs for the various trail guides, except where free, are omitted due to inevitable price changes. Write the respective publishers for their latest prices and handling charges.

For a listing of these and other regional bicycle guides, see *The Cyclists' Yellow Pages*, available from Bikecentennial, P.O. Box 8308, Missoula, MT 59807.

MULTIREGIONAL

East Coast Bicycle Trail. Strip maps of suggested routes in eleven eastern Atlantic states. Packaged in sections: Boston to Philadelphia, Philadelphia to Richmond, Richmond to Savannah. Available from East Coast Bicycle Congress, 333 East 25th Street, Baltimore, MD 21218.

Southwest America Bicycle Trail. A 1,707-mile route that travels through southern California, Arizona, New Mexico, Texas, and Oklahoma. The route meets the Trans-America Bicycle Trail in Larned, Kansas. Map and guide available from YMCA, 816 Van Buren, Amarillo, TX 79101.

Trans-America Bicycle Trail. Strip maps and guidebooks for a 4,250-mile trail from Astoria, Oregon, to Yorktown, Virginia. The maps and guidebooks are published in five sections: Coast-Cascades, Rocky Mountains, Plains-Ozarks, Bluegrass, and Appalachians. Available from Bikecentennial, P.O. Box 8308, Missoula, MT 59807.

NORTHEAST

Boston-Cape Cod Bikeway. Foldout strip maps of a route from Boston to Provincetown, with a spur route to Woods Hole. Here, ferry connections can be made with Martha's Vineyard and Nantucket. Available from Central Planning Transportation Staff, 27 School Street, Boston, MA 02108 (free).

French Connection Bicycle Route. Strip maps detailing north-south routes from Poughkeepsie, New York, and Hartford, Connecticut, to Montreal. Available from Jay Anderson, 108 Linwood Ave., Ardmore, PA 19003.

Virginia Loop Bicycle Trail. Strip maps of a 570-mile route that travels through Washington, DC; Harpers Ferry, West Virginia; the Blue Ridge Mountains; and Charlottesville and Fredericksburg, Virginia. Available from Bikecentennial, P.O. Box 8308, Missoula, MT 59807.

SOUTHEAST

Georgia Bikeways. Strip maps of a 300-mile route from southwest Georgia near Jakin to North Carolina. Available from State of Georgia, Dept. of Industry and Trade, 1400 N. Omni International, P.O. Box 1776, Atlanta, GA 30301 (free).

North Carolina Bicycling Highways, Mountains to Sea Bicycle Route. Strip maps of a 700-mile route from Murphy in the Appalachians to Manteo on the Atlantic Ocean. Available from Bicycle Program, North Carolina Dept. of Transportation, P.O. Box 25201, Raleigh, NC 27611 (free).

North Carolina Bicycling Highways, Piedmont Spur Bicycle Route. Strip maps of a 214-mile spur trail off the Mountains to Sea Bicycle Route. Available from Bicycle Program, North Carolina Dept. of Transportation, P.O. Box 25201, Raleigh, NC 27611 (free).

MIDWEST & GREAT LAKES

Cardinal Trail. Strip maps of a 310-mile east-west route across Ohio. The route travels from near Richmond, Indiana, to northeast Ohio near Youngstown. Available from Columbus Council–AYH, c/o Ed Honton, 1719 Eddystone Ave., Columbus, OH 43224.

Kentucky Loop Bicycle Trail. Strip map of a loop trail that should be used in conjunction with the Bluegrass section map and guide of the Trans-America Bicycle Trail. Available from Bikecentennial, P.O. Box 8308, Missoula, MT 59807.

Wisconsin Bikeway. Strip maps of a 300-mile route from Kenosha on Lake Michigan to La Crosse. Available from Vacation & Travel

Service, Wisconsin Dept. of Natural Resources, Box 450, Madison, WI 54701 (free).

Wisconsin North-South Bikeway. Strip maps of a 300-mile route from Bayfield to La Crosse. Available from Vacation & Travel Service, Wisconsin Dept. of Natural Resources, Box 450, Madison, WI 54701 (free).

NORTHERN PLAINS

Great River Bicycle Route North. Strip maps of an 880-mile trail from Fargo, North Dakota, to Davenport, Iowa, paralleling much of the upper Mississippi River. Available from Bikecentennial, P.O. Box 8308, Missoula, MT 59807. A southern extension is planned.

SOUTHERN PLAINS

Lone Star Bicycle Route. Foldout map of a 950-mile route that travels from Louisiana to the Southwest America Bicycle Trail in Amarillo, Texas. Available from State Dept. of Highways and Public Transportation, Travel and Information Division, P.O. Box 5064, Austin, TX 78763 (free).

SOUTHWEST

Colorado Front Range Bicycle Route. Strip maps of a 300-mile route from Raton Pass on the New Mexico border to the Wyoming border south of Cheyenne. Available from Public Relations, Room 235, Colorado Dept. of Highways, 4201 E. Arkansas Ave., Denver, CO 80222 (free).

Colorado Across the Rockies Bicycle Route. A bicycle route from Denver to the Utah border. Available from Public Relations, Room 235, Colorado Dept. of Highways, 4201 E. Arkansas Ave., Denver, CO 80222 (free).

Colorado Over the Plains Bicycle Route. A bicycle route from Denver to the Kansas border. Available from Public Relations, Room 235, Colorado Dept. of Highways, 4201 E. Arkansas Ave., Denver, CO 80222 (free).

Colorado South Platte Bicycle Route. A bicycle route from Denver to the Nebraska border. Available from Public Relations, Room 235, Colorado Dept. of Highways, 4201 E. Arkansas Ave., Denver, CO 80222 (free).

Great Parks Bicycle Route South. Strip maps of a 775-mile trail linking major parks in the central and southern Rockies between Steamboat Springs, Colorado, and Santa Fe, New Mexico. Available from Bikecentennial, P.O. Box 8308, Missoula, MT 59807.

NORTHWEST

Great Parks Bicycle Route North. Strip maps of a 700-mile trail linking major parks in the northern Rockies between Missoula, Montana, and Jasper, Alberta. Available from Bikecentennial, P.O. Box 8308, Missoula, MT 59807.

Oregon Bike Routes. Foldout map showing bike routes in Oregon, including the Trans-America Bicycle Trail and the Pacific Coast Bicycle Route. Available from Oregon Dept. of Transportation, Travel Information Section, 101 Transportation Bldg., Salem, OR 97310 (free).

Oregon Loop Bicycle Trail. Strip map of a loop trail that travels through Portland, Astoria, and the Willamette Valley in Oregon. The loop follows part of the Trans-America Bicycle Trail. Available from Bikecentennial, P.O. Box 8308, Missoula, MT 59807.

Washington State Bike Book. Index folder describing strip maps available for bicycle routes in Washington State, including the Pacific Coast Bicycle Route. Available from Highway Development, Dept. of Transportation, Highway Administration Bldg., Olympia, WA 98504 (free).

CALIFORNIA

Pacific Coast Bicycle Route—California. Strip maps of a 1,000-mile route that parallels the California coastline from Mexico to Oregon. Available from Caltrans, 6002 Folsom Blvd., Sacramento, CA 95819.

LOW-COST ACCOMMODATIONS

Accommodations for the bicycle tourist might consist of a simple hostel, primitive campsite, university dorm, budget motel, or even a friendly home. If you are traveling alone or with one or two other people, advance reservations are not always necessary. If you wish to make use of hospitality homes listed in the various directories, or plan to travel through popular parklands, by all means write or call ahead.

To save weight, choose only those directories you feel will be most helpful for your particular trip. Then, Xerox only those pages that pertain to the area you will visit. You can carry these sheets with ease. Costs for the various directories listed below are omitted due to inevitable price changes. Write each publisher for their latest prices and handling charges.

HOSTELS

More than 240 hostels serve outdoor travelers in the United States. Hostels provide bunks, usually a kitchen where users can prepare their own meals, and usually a hot shower. Some hostels provide special accommodations for families. Hostelers must be members of American Youth Hostels (AYH) or of the International Youth Hostel Federation (IYHF). Foreign visitors who do not hold a card issued by their home country can purchase an International Guest Card (Foreign National Card) for use in the U.S. Overnight fees at hostels range from about $3 to $6 per night. Large city hostels generally charge more than $5 per night.

Write American Youth Hostels, National Organization, 1332 "I" St., NW, 8th Floor, Washington, DC 20005. For information on Canadian hostels, write Canadian Hosteling Association, 333 River Rd., Vanier City, Ottawa, Ontario, Canada K1L 8B9.

HOSPITALITY HOMES

The following groups have organized home hospitality systems in the United States for traveling bicyclists.

League of American Wheelmen (LAW), 10 East Read St., P.O. Box 988, Baltimore, MD 21203. Volunteers provide a place to sleep for the night free of charge, and sometimes provide breakfast for the traveling bicyclist. The hospitality list is for LAW members only.

Touring Cyclists' Hospitality Directory, by John Mosley, 13623 Sylvan, Van Nuys, CA 91401. A listing of persons who have volunteered to extend simple hospitality—a place to stay and a shower—to touring bicyclists. This is a cooperative venture by some 700 people; the list is available only by volunteering your own home in exchange. The only exception to this rule is for foreign cyclists travelling in America, who may write for a free copy without any obligation.

GENERAL ACCOMMODATIONS

Universities, budget motels, YMCAs, and guest houses.

America on $8 to $16 A Night, by Bob & Ellen Christopher, A Travel Discoveries Publication, P.O. Box 47, Milford, CT 06460. 1,500 budget motels and 3,000 restaurants in all fifty states and Canada.

Guide to Guest Houses & Tourist Homes USA, by Betty Rundback, Tourist House Associates of America, Inc., P.O. Box 355-A, Greentown, PA 18426. Private residences in thirty-six coast-to-coast states where owners rent their spare bedrooms to travelers.

Let' Go: USA, by Harvard Student Agencies, E. P. Dutton, 2 Park Av , New York, NY 10016. What to see and do, where to eat and sl ep; covers major cities and national parks.

Where to Stay USA, Council on International Educational Exchange (CIEE), 777 United Nations Plaza, New York, NY 10017. State-by-state listings of more than 1,500 places to spend the night; expanded coverage of most major cities.

CAMPGROUNDS

Campgrounds offer varied facilities for the touring bicyclist. Developed commercial campgrounds generally provide showers, laundry facilities, a small camp store, and maybe even a swimming pool. These campgrounds generally cater to the recreational vehicle campers, so specify that you are a bicycle tourist and would like a tent site. Fees here can range from $3 to over $7 for a single site.

Campgrounds in state parks, national parks, and national forests usually provide excellent sites for tent campers. Modern toilet facilities are sometimes available, and site fees for the bicycle tourist may range from free to about $4. State park campgrounds and national forest campgrounds are especially busy on summer weekends, and national park campgrounds are busy throughout the summer season. You should plan to arrive at these sites early in the day, or make reservations in advance if possible.

The following directories and addresses provide more specific information on campgrounds across the nation.

Camping in the National Park System, U.S. Government Printing Office, Washington, DC 20402 (stock #024-005-00668).

Forest Service, U.S. Department of Agriculture, Washington, DC 20250. Request information for specific national forests.

KOA Camper's Atlas, Kampgrounds of America, Box 30558, Billings, MT 59114.

Rand McNally Campground & Trailer Park Guide, The Western Campgrounds & Trailer Parks Guide, The Eastern Campgrounds & Trailer Parks Guide, Rand McNally & Co., Campground Publications, P.O. Box 728, Skokie, IL 60076.

Camping Around the Appalachian Mountains, Camping Around California, Camping Around New England, Camping Around Washington, Random House, Inc., 201 East 50th St., New York, NY 10022.

EQUIPMENT FOR YOU AND YOUR BIKE

The lists that follow provide addresses for equipment manufacturers and mail-order houses nationwide. These lists can help in your research and selection of quality cycle touring equipment. They cannot, however, replace the convenience, service, and personal attention you can expect from your local bicycle shop or camping store. Inform yourself about the equipment you plan to buy and then shop around. A reasonable price and a good service policy are not too much to ask for.

Unless they are specifically identified as mail-order houses, the manufacturers listed below will usually only provide literature on their products to better inform you. Many mail-order houses charge a fee for their catalog. Write for more information.

BICYCLE PARTS, CLOTHING & ACCESSORIES

Bellwether
1161 Mission St.
San Francisco, CA 94103
(cycle packs and clothing)

Bikecology
P.O. Box 1880
Santa Monica, CA 90406
(mail-order catalog)

Bike Warehouse
215 Main St.
New Middletown, OH 44442
(mail-order catalog)

Cannondale Corp.
35 Pulaski St.
Stamford, CT 06902
(cycle packs and clothing)

Cycle Goods Corp.
2735 Hennepin Ave., So.
Minneapolis, MN 55408
(mail-order catalog)

Eclipse, Inc.
P.O. Box 7370
Ann Arbor, MI 48107
(cycle packs)

Jim Blackburn Designs
1080 Florence Way

Campbell, CA 95008
(cycle racks)

Kirtland Tourpak
Box 4059
Boulder, CO 80306
(cycle packs)

Lickton's Cycle City
310 Lake St.
Oak Park, IL 60302
(mail-order catalog)

Metropolitan New York
    Council–AYH
132 Spring St.
New York, NY 10012
(mail-order catalog)

Palo Alto Bicycles
P.O. Box 1276
Palo Alto, CA 94302
(mail-order catalog)

Touring Cyclist Shop
P.O. Box 4009
2639 Spruce St.
Boulder, CO 80306
(cycle packs and mail-order
    catalog)

SAFETY EQUIPMENT

American Youth Hostels
National Organization
1332 "I" St., NW 8th Floor
Washington, DC 20005
(mail-order fanny bumpers)

Bell Helmets, Inc.
15301 Shoemaker Ave.
Norwalk, CA 90650
(cycle helmets)

Bicycle Lighting Systems
718 N. Vermont St.
Arlington, VA 22203
(mail-order bike lights)

Bike Security Systems
177 Tosca Dr.
Stoughton, MA 02072
(Citadel bike locks)

Ultra Light Shop
Quarry Chapel Rd. at Wiggin
Gambier, OH 43022
(mail-order cyclist mirrors)

KBL Corporation
95 Freeport St.
Boston, MA 02122
(Kryptonite bike locks)

Mountain Safety Research
 (MSR)
631 S. 96th St.
Seattle, WA 98108
(cycle helmets)

Pro-tec, Inc.
11108 Northrup Way
Bellevue, WA 98004
(cycle helmets)

Safety Sport Mirror, Inc.
Box 214
Chardon, OH 44024
(mail-order cyclist mirrors)

Skid-Lid Manufacturing Co.
650 4th Ave.
San Diego, CA 92101
(cycle helmets)

CAMPING GEAR

Early Winters, Ltd.
110 Prefontaine Pl., So.
Seattle, WA 98104
(mail-order catalog)

Eastern Mountain Sports, Inc.
 (EMS)
Vose Farm Rd.
Peterborough, NH 03458
(mail-order catalog)

Eddie Bauer
P.O. Box 3700

Fifth & Union
Seattle, WA 98124
(mail-order catalog)

Frostline Kits
452 Burbank
Broomfield, CO 80022
(mail-order kits)

Holubar Mountaineering
P.O. Box 7
Boulder, CO 80306
(mail-order catalog)

L. L. Bean, Inc.
Freeport, ME 04033
(mail-order catalog)

The North Face
1234 Fifth St.
Berkeley, CA 94710
(tents, packs, and sleeping
  bags)

Recreational Equipment, Inc.
  (REI)
P.O. Box C-88125
Seattle, WA 98188
(mail-order catalog)

NATIONAL BICYCLING ORGANIZATIONS & AYH COUNCILS

The several organizations listed below play an active role in the promotion of bicycle touring, bicycle safety, and bicycle racing nationwide. You may choose to join those identified as membership organizations.

American Youth Hostels (AYH)
National Organization
1332 "I" St., NW, 8th Floor
Washington, DC 20005

Membership organization. Oversees a system of more than 240 hostels nationwide. Sponsors European and domestic bicycle trips for teen-agers and adults. More than thirty local Councils have active outdoor programs and provide various services to members (see addresses listed below). Quarterly newsletter: *The Knapsack*.

Bicycle Manufacturers Assoc. of America (BMA)
1101 15th St., NW
Washington, DC 20005

Represents about 80 percent of domestic manufacturers. Its members finance major programs that cut across the fields of politics, public safety, transportation, trade and tariff, community and government relations, consumerism, and much more. Newsletter: *Boom in Bikeways*.

Bikecentennial
P.O. Box 8308
Missoula, MT 59807

Membership organization. The national service organization for touring bicyclists. Bikecentennial is devoted to the research and development of public bicycle recreation facilities and programs nationwide. A large part of the organization's efforts go into producing and mapping touring routes for cyclists, in order to promote and encourage an appreciation of America through healthful bicycle travel. Bimonthly newsletter: *BikeReport*.

League of American Wheelman (LAW)
10 East Read St.
P.O. Box 988
Baltimore, MD 21203

Membership organization. An organization of American cyclists promoting and defending the rights of bicyclists. Encourages safe cycling, lobbies for safe roads, holds large regional rallies, and promotes bicycle touring. Also encourages and guides bicycle clubs and promotes their activities. Monthly magazine: *American Wheelman*.

United States Cycling Federation (USCF)
1750 E. Boulder St.
Colorado Springs, CO 80909

Membership organization. The national amateur bicycle racing organization.

AYH COUNCILS

Northeast
Greater Boston Council
251 Harvard St.
Brookline, MA 02146

Hartford Area Council
P.O. Box 10392
Elmwood, CT 06110

Metropolitan New York
 Council
132 Spring St.
New York, NY 10012

Northern New York Council
42 W. Main St.
Malone, NY 12953

Syracuse Council
459 Westcott St.
Syracuse, NY 13210

Mid-Atlantic
Delaware Valley Council
35 S. Third St.
Philadelphia, PA 19103

Pittsburgh Council
6300 Fifth St.
Pittsburgh, PA 15232

Potomac Area Council
1520 16th St., NW
Washington, DC 20036

Midwest & Great Lakes
Metropolitan Chicago Council
3712 North Clark St.
Chicago, IL 60613

Columbus Council
125 Amazon Place
Columbus, OH 43209

Metropolitan Detroit Council
3024 Coolidge
Berkley, MI 48072

Erie-Ana Council
304 N. Church St.
Bowling Green, OH 43402

Lima Council
P.O. Box 173
Lima, OH 45802

Northwest Indiana Council
8231 Lake Shore Dr.
Gary, IN 46403

Toledo Area Council
3440 Lawrin Dr.
Toledo, OH 43623

Tri-State Council
5400 Lanius Lane
Cincinnati, OH 45224

Western Michigan Council
6421 Station C
Grand Rapids, MI 49509

Wisconsin Council
7218 West North Ave.
Wauwatosa, WI 52313

Northern Plains
Minnesota Council
475 Cedar St.
St. Paul, MN 55101

Nebraskaland Council
Wesley House
640 N. 16th St.
Lincoln, NE 68508

Northeast Iowa Council
P.O. Box 10
Postville, IA 52162

Southern Plains
Ozark Area Council
5400 A Southwest
St. Louis, MO 63139

Northwest
Washington State Council
1431 Minor Ave.
Seattle, WA 98101

Southwest
Arizona State Council
14049 N. 38th Place
Phoenix, AZ 85032

Rocky Mountain Council
1107 12th St.
Boulder, CO 80306

California
Central California Council
P.O. Box 28148
San Jose, CA 95159

Golden Gate Council
Bldg. 240, Fort Mason
San Francisco, CA 94123

San Diego Council
1031 India St.
San Diego, CA 92101

Los Angeles Council
1502 Palos Verdes Dr., North
Harbor City, CA 90710

For a list of new Councils and Council address changes, write *American Youth Hostels, National Organization, 1332 "I" St., NW, 8th Floor, Washington, DC 20005.*

PART TWO
Bicycle Tours

READING THE ROUTE MAPS & DESCRIPTIONS

The bike trips that follow have been divided into nine geographical regions:

Northeast: Maine, New Hampshire, Vermont, Massachusetts, Connecticut, Rhode Island, New York.

Mid-Atlantic: Pennsylvania, New Jersey, Maryland, Delaware, District of Columbia, Virginia, West Virginia.

Southeast: North Carolina, South Carolina, Tennessee, Mississippi, Alabama, Georgia, Florida.

Midwest & Great Lakes: Ohio, Indiana, Illinois, Kentucky, Michigan, Wisconsin.

Northern Plains: Minnesota

Southern Plains: Louisiana, Arkansas, Texas, Oklahoma, Kansas, Missouri.

Northwest: Idaho, Montana, Washington, Oregon.

Southwest: Colorado, Utah, New Mexico, Arizona, Nevada.

California.

Three types of bicycle tours are described in *The American Bicycle Atlas*. Short half-day and day trips are included and cover urban and park areas in or near major population centers. These routes are presented to encourage the less experienced biker as well as the biker who doesn't have time for a longer tour. Longer day trips and weekend trips in rural areas will encourage bikers to spend more time on the road without committing themselves to extensive planning and preparation. Finally, extended tours of from two to nine days are presented for the vacationing bicycle tourist. Many of these longer tours require advance planning to locate and reserve overnight accommodations.

All the bicycle trips presented make use of existing secondary roads, state highways, U.S. highways, and designated bicycle paths. Congested areas have been avoided where possible, and unpaved roads have been kept to a minimum. Nevertheless, these roads have been used where they link up lengthy rural sections of back-road bike trips. Be aware that road conditions will vary with both weather and maintenance.

Bike trip starting points have generally been located near overnight parking facilities or near public transportation (plane, train, or bus service). In some cases overnight automobile parking may be a problem, and an alternate starting point will have to be chosen.

Each bike trip begins with a standard description, presented as follows:

Tour Name & Number: the numbers are keyed to the regional maps that begin each section.

Counties and States: these give the area through which the trip travels; you may refer to Chapter 3 for agencies to contact for detailed supplemental maps.

Length: given in miles; all mileages are approximate.

Terrain: these are rated as follows:
> Very Hilly—many long, steep hills
> Hilly—long, steep hills mixed with smaller hills
> Rolling Hills—smaller hills, none of great difficulty
> Level—mostly flat, with only occasional hills

Points of Interest: national parks, historic sites, good eating places, places to swim, etc.

Special Notes: any other appropriate information for a specific trip.

This standard trip description is followed by detailed route directions that should be used in conjunction with the route maps. "R" means a right turn and "L" means a left turn. Appropriate comments, such as hilly spots, gravel roads, and directional landmarks, are also included.

MAP SYMBOLS

 Arrow points north

 U.S. highway

(351) State or county highway

1 Services: where you will find public transportation, motels, hostels, food services and bike shops along a route. The number on the map is keyed to the route text. No effort has been made to list all the services available on a particular trip. Addresses are given where available.

 Campground: the number is used and keyed to the text only when the campground name is known. Otherwise, the symbol is used but no number is printed. Addresses are given where available.

 Points of interest

Trip mileages are listed in miles (*mi*) and in kilometers (*km*) in the lower corner of each map; all mileages are approximate.

CHAPTER FOUR
Northeast

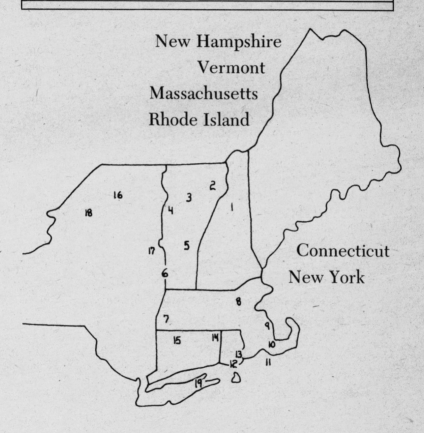

New Hampshire
Vermont
Massachusetts
Rhode Island

Connecticut
New York

White Mountains Tour (#1)

GRAFTON, CARROLL, AND COOS COUNTIES, NEW HAMPSHIRE

Length: *113 miles*

Terrain: *Hilly*

Points of Interest: *White Mountains, Kancamagus Highway, old covered bridges*

1 Start in North Conway on US 302 in eastern New Hampshire/motels; food services
  Go north on US 302/uphill to Crawford Notch

2 Covered Bridge

3 Crawford Notch (el. 1,773 ft.)

4 Crawford Notch State Park

5 Zealand Campground
  L–US 3 at Twin Mountain
  Bear R–Route 141/continue past I-93
  R–Route 18
  L–Route 116 at Franconia
  L–Route 112 uphill to Kinsman Notch

6 Wildwood Campground

7 Kinsman Notch (el. 1,814 ft.)

8 Covered Bridge

9 Lincoln/food services
  Continue east on Kancamagus Highway (Route 112)/uphill to Kancamagus Pass

10 Big Rock Campground

11 Kancamagus Pass (el. 2,860 ft.)

12 Passaconaway Campground

13 Jigger Johnson Campground

14 Blackberry Crossing Campground

15 Covered Bridge Campground
   L–Route 16

16 Covered Bridges

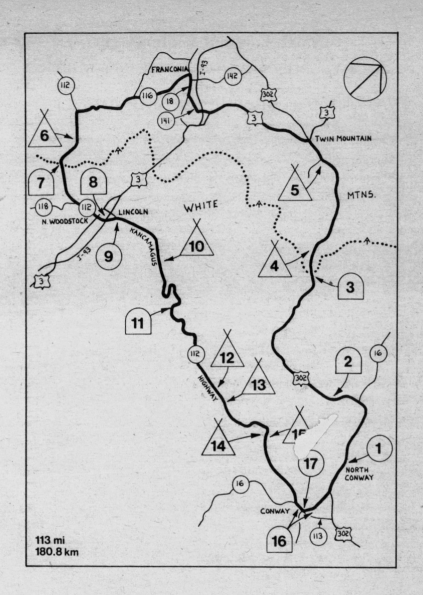

17 Conway/food services
Continue north on Route 16 and US 302
Return to North Conway

North Vermont Venture (#2)

Length: *165 miles*

Terrain: *Hilly*

Points of Interest: *northern Vermont countryside, Connecticut River*

1　Start at St. Johnsbury/bus service; motels; food services; bike shop
　Go west on US 2
　R–to North Danville
　R–continue on US 2 at Danville
　R–Route 15
　R–Route 16

2　Barton/food services

3　Crystal Lake State Park
　L–Route 5A at Lake Willoughby
　Continue north on Routes 5A & 105

4　Derby Center/food services

5　Char-Bo Campground
　R–Route 111 at Derby Center

6　Island Pond/food services
　Continue east on Route 105

7　Brighton State Park
　R–Route 102 at Bloomfield

8　Maidstone State Forest
　L–US 2

9　Lancaster, N.H./food services
　R–Route 135 at Lancaster

10　Littleton/food services
　R–Route 18 at Littleton
　Bear L (west)–US 2
　Return to St. Johnsbury

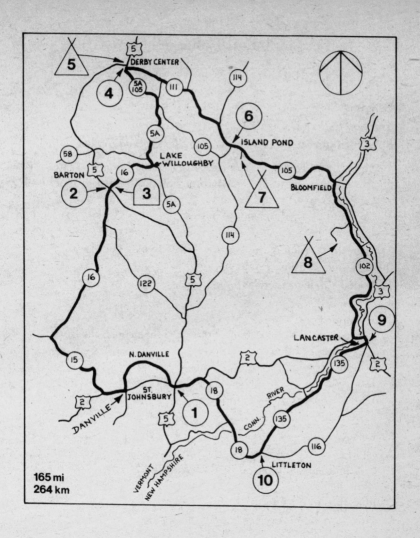

165 mi
264 km

Vermont Fall Foliage Tour (#3)

WASHINGTON COUNTY, VERMONT

Length: *55 miles*
Terrain: *Rolling Hills to Hilly*
Points of Interest: *Mad River, waterfalls, covered bridges*

1　Start in Waterbury Center/Ski Hostel Lodge, Waterbury Center, VT 05677; north from I-89 on Route 100 about four miles to signs for hostel
　Go south on road in front of hostel
　L–Route 100
2　Waterbury/train & bus service; food services
　Continue south on Route 100
3　Waitsfield/food services
4　Covered Bridge
　R–Route 17
　L–access road to Sugarbush North and Sugarbush ski areas
　L–at T-intersection
　R–Route 100
　L–to Warren
　L–to East Warren/long uphill
5　Covered Bridge
6　East Warren/food services
7　Old Homestead Hostel/Box 118, Warren, VT 05674
　Continue north on paved road to Waitsfield
　R–Route 100
　Bear R–Route 100B
8　Moretown/food services
　L–US 2 at Middlesex
9　Middlesex/food services
　R–Route 100 at Waterbury
　Return to Waterbury Center

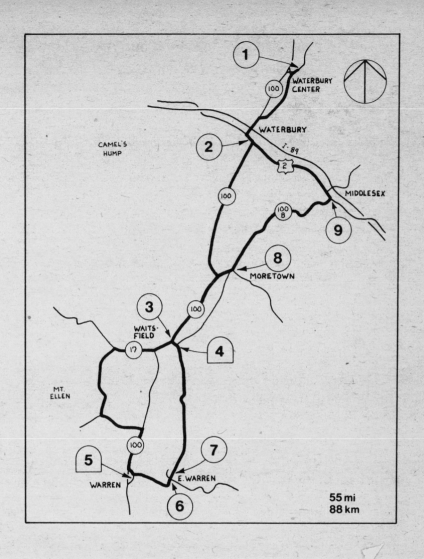

55 mi
88 km

Middlebury–Lake Champlain Tour (#4)

ADDISON COUNTY, VERMONT

Length: *47 miles*

Terrain: *Level*

Points of Interest: *D.A.R. State Park, Button Bay State Park, Lake Champlain, Morgan Horse Farm, State Craft Center*

Special Note: *Middlebury is an alternate starting point*

1 Start at D.A.R. State Park
  L–Lake St.
  R–Pease Rd.
  L–Jersey St. at T-intersection
  L–at fork onto Sherman Rd./becomes Button Bay Rd.

2 Button Bay State Park
  R–Basin Harbor Rd. at T-intersection
  L–at stop sign onto unsigned road
  L–West Main St. (Route 22A North)

3 Vergennes/food services
  R–unsigned road between Enis Portraits and Gallery Restaurant
  Continue straight across intersection at stop sign
  R–Route 17 West at stop sign
  L–Route 23 South
  L–Hamilton Rd. just after Weybridge Congregational Church/
      unpaved
  R–at T-intersection onto paved and unsigned road

4 Morgan Horse Farm
  L–at traffic island/through covered bridge

5 Cov d Bridge/only double-lane covered bridge still in use in
      Vermont
  L–through underpass after Barnera's Florist
  R–unsigned road opposite Stan's Shop and Save Market at
      Middlebury

6 Middlebury/bus service; motels; food services; bike shop
  R–Route 125 West
  R–continue west on Route 125 at Bridport
  L–Route 125 West at Pratt's Store
  R–at Chimney Point
  Return to D.A.R. State Park

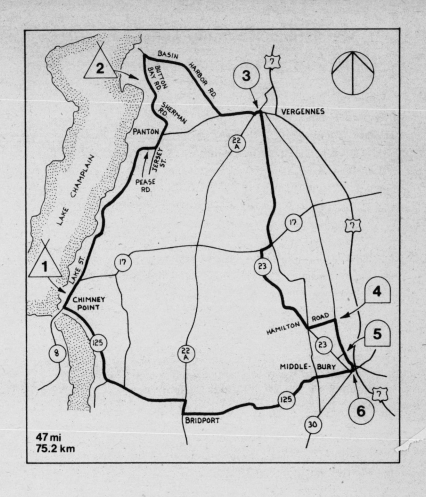

47 mi
75.2 km

Green Mountain Tour (#5)

BENNINGTON, RUTLAND, AND WINDSOR COUNTIES, VERMONT

Lentgh: *146 miles*

Terrain: *Hilly*

Points of Interest: *Green Mountains, Killington Gondola Ride, historic Woodstock, Queechee Gorge*

Special Notes: *Rutland and White River Jct. are alternate starting points; food services are located in most towns on this tour.*

1 Start at Ludlow Youth Hostel/44 Pleasant St., Ludlow, VT 05149; but service; food services; bike shop
   Go south on Route 100
   R (west)–Route 11 at Londonderry; hard climb over Green Mountains
   Continue west on Routes 11 & 30 to Manchester Center

2 Manchester Depot and Manchester Center/motels; food services
   Continue on Route 30 at Manchester Center
   R–Route 133 at Pawlet
   R–Routes 133 & 140 at Middletown Springs
   L–Route 133
   R (east)–US 4 at W. Rutland

3 Rutland/bus service; motels; food services; bike shops
   Continue east on US 4/hard climb over Sherburne Pass

4 Sherburne Pass (el. 2,190 ft.)

5 Gifford Woods State Park

6 Sherburne Center/motels; food services

7 Killington Ski Area Gondola/operates year-round

8 Woodstock/motels; food services
   R–Route 12

9 Queechee Recreation Area

10 White Riber Jct./train & bus service; motels; food services; bike shops
   R (south)–US 5
   R (west)–Route 131 at Ascutney

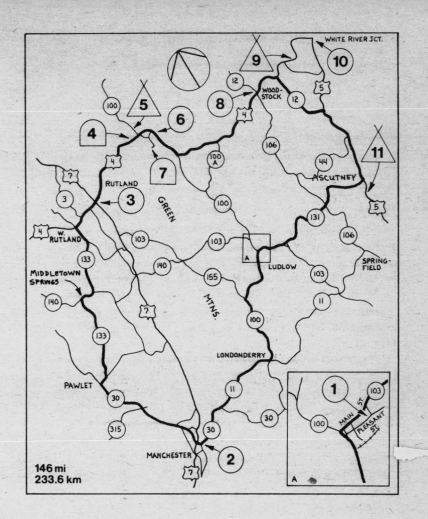

11 Wilgus State Park
   Continue west on Route 103
   Return to Ludlow

Bennington–Battenkill River Tour (#6)

BENNINGTON COUNTY, VERMONT
RENSSELAER AND WASHINGTON COUNTIES, NEW YORK

Length: *55 miles*

Terrain: *Rolling Hills*

Points of Interest: *Old Bennington and Bennington Battlefield, Battenkill River*

1   Start at Old Bennington on Route 9 west of Bennington
    Go east on W. Main St. (Route 9)
2   Bennington/bus service; motels; food services; bike shop
    L–Benmont Av.
    L–Northside Dr. to Route 67A and North Bennington
    North on Route 67 at North Bennington
    L (north)–Route 7A
    Continue north on US 7 into Arlington
3   Arlington/food services
    L (west)–Route 313/along Battenkill River into New York State
4   Cambridge, N.Y./food services
    L (south)–Route 22
    Bear L (east)–Routes 22 & 67
    Continue east on Route 67 at North Hoosik
    R (south)–Route 67A at North Bennington
    Continue on Northside Dr.
    Bear R–Benmont Av.
    R–W. Main St.
    Return to Old Bennington

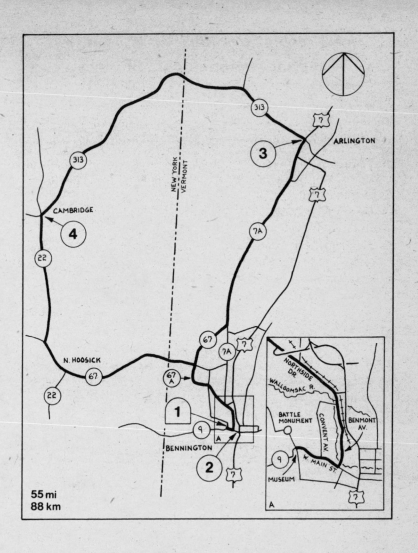

Stockbridge–Housatonic River Tour (#7)

BERKSHIRE COUNTY, MASSACHUSETTS

Length: *37 miles*
Terrain: *Hilly*
Points of Interest: *Housatonic River, covered bridges, Berkshires*

1 Start at Mount Everett Youth Hostel/Rt. 1, Box 161, Sheffield,
    MA 01257; west of US 7 and Sheffield off Berkshire School
    Rd. on Route 41
    Go north on Route 41
    R–Berkshire School Rd.

2 Sheffield/food service
    L–US 7 at Sheffield

3 Covered Bridge/3.5 miles off US 7

4 Covered Bridge

5 Great Barrington/food services

6 Stockbridge/food services
    L–Glendale Middle Rd. at Stockbridge
    L–Route 183
    R–Main St. at Housatonic
    L–Route 41
    Continue west on Routes 23 & 41 at Great Barrington
    L–Route 41 at S. Egremont
    Return to Mount Everett Youth Hostel

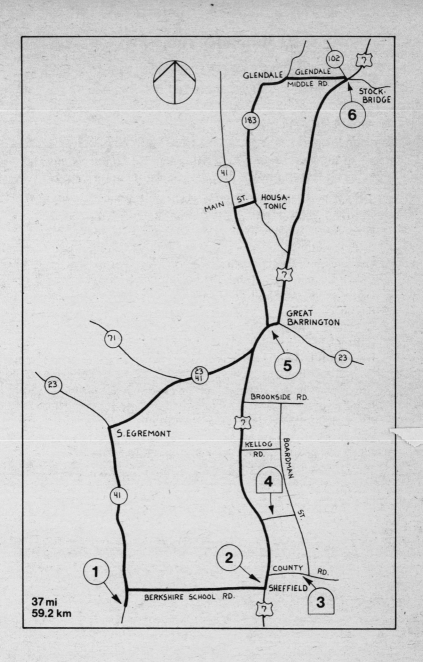

GLENDALE
GLENDALE
MIDDLE RD.
102
7
STOCK-
BRIDGE
183
6
41
MAIN ST. HOUSA-
TONIC
7
GREAT
BARRINGTON
71
23
5
23
41
BROOKSIDE RD.
23
7
S. EGREMONT
KELLOG RD.
BOARDMAN
4
41
ST.
2
COUNTY RD.
SHEFFIELD
1
BERKSHIRE SCHOOL RD.
3
7
37 mi
59.2 km

Minuteman Tour (#8)

SUFFOLK, MIDDLESEX, AND WORCESTER COUNTIES, MASSACHUSETTS

Length: *16 miles one way*
Terrain: *Rolling Hills*
Points of Interest: *historic Concord, roads the Minutemen took to the battle at Old North Bridge in Concord on April 19, 1775*

1   Start at Friendly Crossways Youth Hostel/Whitcomb Av., Littleton, MA 01460; near I-495 and Route 2 intersection
    Go north on Whitcomb Av.
    R–Taylor St.
    Continue on Liberty Square Rd.
    L–Massachusetts Av. (Route 111)
    L fork–Arlington St. at West Acton
    R–Hayward Rd.
    L–Main St. (Route 27) to Acton Center
    R–Brook St.
    R–Great Rd. (Route 2A)/busy road
    Continue to Rotary Circle
    Cross street before Rotary Circle and continue clockwise
    L–Barretts Mill Rd.
    Continue on Barnes Hill Rd. at Route 126
    Bear R–Estabrook Rd.

2   Minute Man National Park/information center

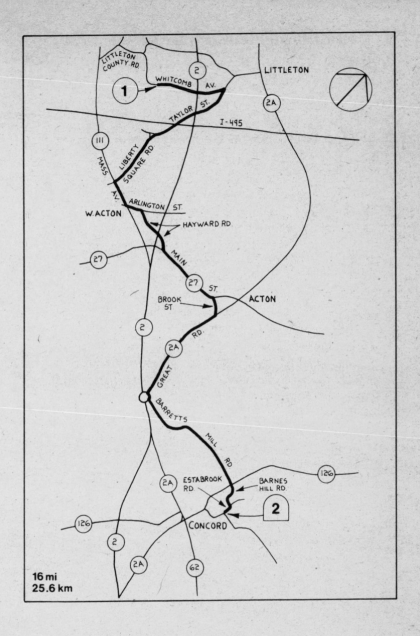

East Bridgewater to Cedarville (#9)

PLYMOUTH COUNTY, MASSACHUSETTS

Length: *38 miles one way*
Terrain: *Rolling Hills*
Points of Interest: *Train Hostel, historic Plymouth, Cape Cod Bay*

1 Start at the Train Hostel/234 Central St., E. Bridgewater, MA
      02333; south of Boston off Route 28; food services and bike
      shop nearby

2 Brockton/bus service
      Go R (west) on Central St.
      L (south)–Plymouth St.
      Bear L (east)–Route 106
      Continue south on Route 3A at Kingston

3 Plymouth/food services; bike shops; historic settlement
      Bear R–Herring Pond Rd. at Bruno's Store and Gas Station in
         Cedarville/under Route 3

4 Cedarville/food services
      R–Long Pond Rd./first paved road after Route 3
      Bear L–Carter Bridge Rd./Long Pond Rd. becomes gravel
      R–still Carter Bridge Rd.

5 Camp Massasoit Hostel/Sandy Pond Rd., RFD 5, Box 636,
      Plymouth, MA 02360

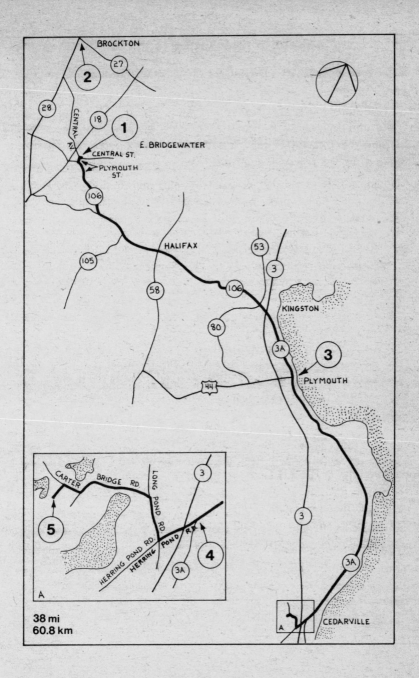

38 mi
60.8 km

Cedarville to Wood's Hole (#10)

BARNSTABLE COUNTY, MASSACHUSETTS

Length: *25 miles one way*
Terrain: *Level*
Points of Interest: *Cape Cod Canal, Wood's Hole, ferries to Martha's Vineyard and Nantucket*

1 Start at the Camp Massasoit Hostel/Sandy Pond Rd., RFD 5, Box 636, Plymouth, MA 02360
  Go east on Carter Bridge Rd.
  L–still Carter Bridge Rd.
  Bear R–Long Pond Rd.
  L–Herring Pond Rd./continue under Route 3
  R (south)–Route 3A at Cedarville; signed bike route continues to Bourne

2 Cedarville/food services
  Bear R at fork to Sagamore Bridge
  Cross Sagamore Bridge on sidewalk
  Continue west on Cape Cod Canal Service Road
  L–leave service road under Bourne Bridge/cross RR tracks
  R–Sandwich Rd.

3 Bourne/food services
  Continue south on County Rd. at six-road intersection in Bourne
  Continue south on Route 28A
  R–at sign to Sippewisset
  R–Sippewisset Rd.
  Bear R–continue on Sippewisset Rd.
  Continue on Quissett Rd.

4 Wood's Hole/motels; food services
  R and then L for ferries to Islands at Wood's Hole

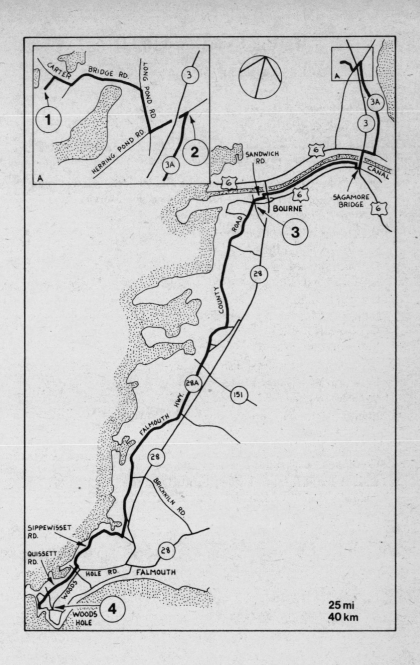

77

Martha's Vineyard (#11)

DUKES COUNTY, MASSACHUSETTS

Length: *48 miles*

Terrain: *Rolling Hills*

Points of Interest: *Gay Head Cliffs, Menemsha Fishing Village, Edgartown historic homes and churches, ocean swimming*

1 Start at Ferry Landing in Vineyard Haven/ferries arrive regularly from Wood's Hole on Cape Cod; food services
R–State Rd. to W. Tisbury Village

2 W. Tisbury Village/food services
Straight on South Rd.
L–South Rd. at Chilmark Cornerway
L–Moshup's Trail

3 Gay Head Cliffs
Return to Chilmark Cornerway
L–toward North Rd.
L–North Rd.

4 Menemsha Village/fresh fish for sale
Return to W. Tisbury Village
R–Edgartown Rd.

5 Manter Memorial Youth Hostel/Edgartown Rd., W. Tisbury, MA 02575
Continue to Edgartown
Continue to Oak Bluffs

6 Oak Bluffs/ferries to Nantucket and Hyannis
Return to Vineyard Haven

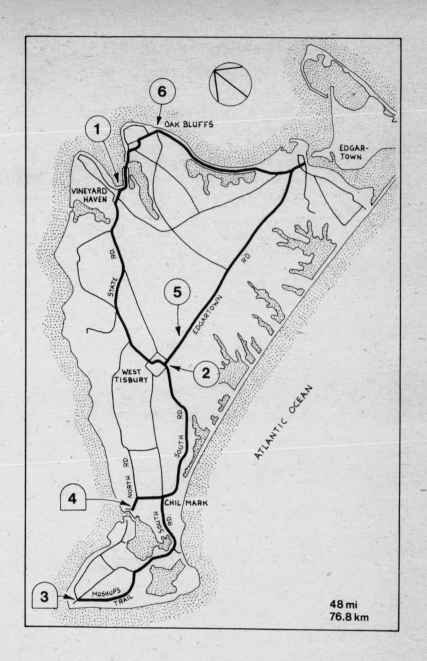

OAK BLUFFS

EDGAR-
TOWN

VINEYARD
HAVEN

STATE RD

EDGARTOWN RD

WEST
TISBURY

SOUTH RD

ATLANTIC OCEAN

NORTH RD

SOUTH RD

CHILMARK

MOSHUPS TRAIL

48 mi
76.8 km

Ocean Drive Tour (#12)

NEWPORT COUNTY, RHODE ISLAND

Length: *10 miles*

Terrain: *Rolling Hills*

Points of Interest: *Fort Adams State Park, Atlantic Ocean, Bretton Point State Park, historic mansions*

Special Note: *Ocean Drive and the mansion area have heavy traffic on summer weekends*

1 Start at Fort Adams State Park southwest of Newport/one of the largest seacoast fortifications built in the U.S., it provides a visual record of military history from the 1800s to the end of World War II

Leave park by main entrance

R–Harrison Av.

R–Ridge Rd.

R–Castle Hill Av.

L–Ocean Av./travel along the rocky shoreline of the Atlantic Ocean

2 Bretton Point State Park

L–Bellevue Av.

3 The Marble House, the Elms, & the Kingscote/historic mansions

L–America's Cup Av.

L–Thames St.

R–Wellington Av.

L–Halidon Av.

R–Harrison Av.

Return to Fort Adams State Park

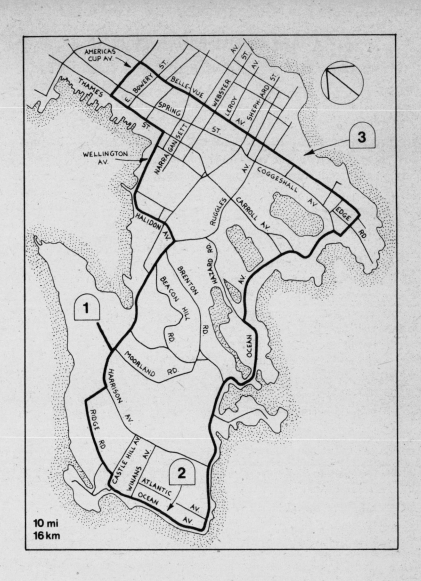

Tiverton–Little Compton Tour (#13)

TIVERTON AND LITTLE COMPTON COUNTIES, RHODE ISLAND

Length: *32 miles*

Terrain: *Level*

Points of Interest: *Sakonnet River and Sakonnet Point, Little Compton, Adamsville*

1 Start at the Stone Bridge Inn on Route 77 in Tiverton/food services
Go south on Route 77 (Main Rd.)
R–Nannaquaket Rd./around Nannaquaket Pond
R–Route 77 (Main Rd.)
R–Seapowet Av.

2 Seapowet Management Area
Bear R (south)–Puncatest Rd.
L–Fogland Rd.
R–Route 77 (Main Rd.)
Continue on Sakonnet Point Rd. to Sakonnet Point

3 Sakonnet Point
Return on Sakonnet Point Rd.
R (east)–Swamp Rd.
L–South Commons Av. to Little Compton
Continue on Willow Av.
R–Peckham Rd.
L–Long Hwy.
R–Cold Brook Rd. to Adamsville

4 Adamsville/food service
L–Stone Church Rd.
Bear R–Lake Rd.
R–King Rd.
L–Brayton Rd.
L–Bulgarmarsh Rd. (Route 177)
R–Route 77 (Main Rd.)
Return to Tiverton

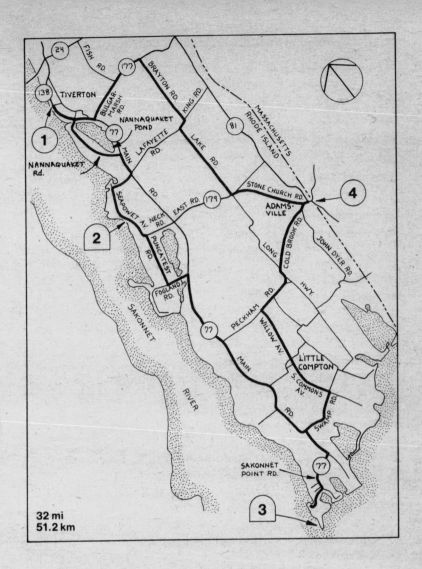

32 mi
51.2 km

Putnam-Woodstock-Thompson Tour (#14)

PUTNAM, WOODSTOCK, AND THOMPSON COUNTIES, CONNECTICUT
GLOUCESTER COUNTY, RHODE ISLAND

Length: *34 miles*

Terrain: *Hilly*

Points of Interest: *Quinebaug River, Quaddick State Park and Reservoir, northeastern Connecticut countryside*

1   Start in Putnam on US 44 just west of Route 52 in northeastern Connecticut/food services
Go west on US 44/caution at short steep hill with traffic light at bottom
R–Sabin Rd.
Bear L–Harrisville Rd.
R–Butts Rd.
L–Route 171
Bear R–Route 169 at S. Woodstock

2   S. Woodstock/food service
Bear R–past Woodstock Academy at Woodstock
R–Childs Hill Rd.
Bear L–onto paved road for .3 mile
Bear L–onto Dugg Hill Rd.
R–Chandler School Rd.
R–Fabyan Rd./along Quinebaug River
L–at West Thompson/pass West Thompson Lake
Straight on Route 193 through Thompson
R–Gawron Rd.
R–Brandy Hill Rd.

3   Quaddick State Park/fishing & swimming
L–Quaddick Rd. at Quaddick

4   Quaddick/food service
R–US 44/for .3 mile
Bear L–Five Mile River Rd.
Bear R–Route 12/just after Route 52
Return to Putnam

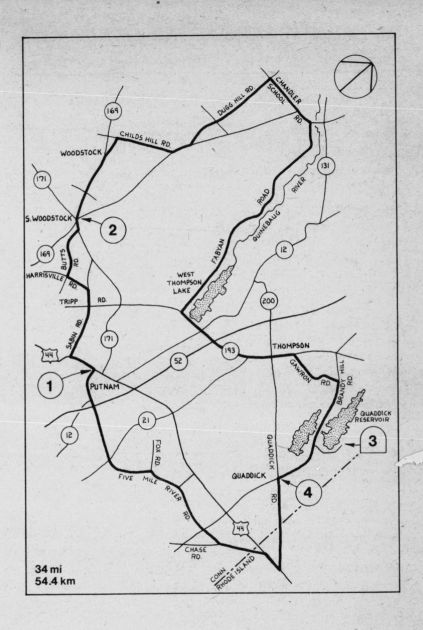

34 mi
54.4 km

Northern Connecticut Tour (#15)

MORRIS, LITCHFIELD, TORRINGTON, NEW HARTFORD,
WINCHESTER, AND
BARKHAMSTED COUNTIES, CONNECTICUT

Length: *56 miles*

Terrain: *Rolling Hills*

Points of Interest: *Bantam Lake, Peoples State Forest, Barkhamsted Reservoir*

1 Start at Bantam Lake Youth Hostel/East Shore Rd., Lakeside,
    CT 06758; southwest of Litchfield near Bantam Lake
  Go R on East Shore Rd.
  L–Alain White Rd. at T-intersection
  R–US 202

2 Litchfield/food services
  Continue on US 202

3 Torrington/food services
  Continue on US 202/long uphill
  L–Route 183
  R–US 44
  Bear L–Route 318/toward Pleasant Valley
  Continue on Route 181 across bridge
  L–unmarked road/after bridge; follow signs to Peoples State
    Forest

4 Peoples State Forest
  Return to Route 181
  L–Route 181/uphill
  R–Route 318/along Barkhamsted Reservoir Dam
  R–Route 219/downhill to New Hartford

5 New Hartford/food services
  Continue on Route 219/uphill
  R–US 202
  Return to Bantam Lake Youth Hostel

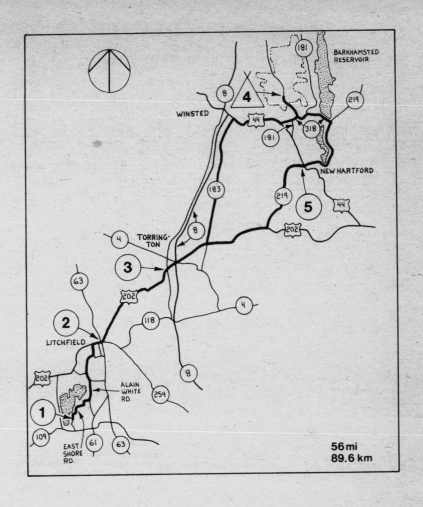

BARKHAMSTED RESERVOIR

181

8

4

WINSTED

44

181

318

219

NEW HARTFORD

183

219

5

44

8

202

4

TORRING-TON

3

63

202

2

118

4

LITCHFIELD

202

ALAIN WHITE RD.

8

1

254

109

EAST SHORE RD.

61

63

56 mi
89.6 km

87

Saint Regis Falls Tour (#16)

FRANKLIN COUNTY, NEW YORK

Length: *40 miles*

Terrain: *Rolling Hills*

Points of Interest: *Saint Regis Falls, Saint Regis River, Meacham Lake*

Special Note: *this tour can be part of a weekend stay at a local campground or at the Rotary Youth Hostel (Keene Mill School House, Paul Smith's, NY 12970), south of Meacham Lake off Route 30*

1   Start at Saint Regis Falls southwest of Malone, NY, on Route 458/motel; food service
Go east on Red Tavern Rd. (Route 14)

2   Food Service
R–Route 30

3   Meacham Lake Campsites
R–Route 458
Return to Saint Regis Falls

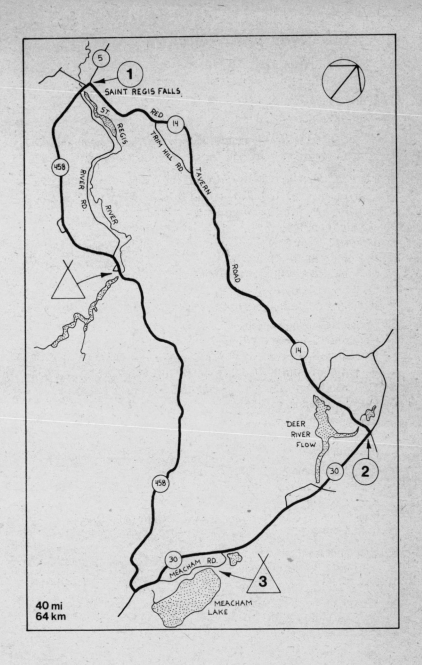

SAINT REGIS FALLS

DEER RIVER FLOW

MEACHAM LAKE

40 mi
64 km

89

Lake George–Warrensburg Tour (#17)

WARREN COUNTY, NEW YORK

Length: *42 miles*

Terrain: *Rolling Hills to Hilly*

Points of Interest: *Chestertown historic district, Bolton Landing town beach, Lake George, Diamond Point Beach*

1 Start at the Glen House Hostel/The Glen, Route 28, Warrensburg, NY 12885; take I-87 exit 23, north on US 9 through Warrensburg, left on Route 28 to hostel
   Go south on Route 28 across Hudson River
   L (north)–County Route 8
   R–County Route 74
   L–County Route 46 to Friends Lake
   Continue on County Route 8
   R–US 9 & State Route 8 to Chestertown

2 Chestertown/food services; historic district; museum
   Continue east on State Route 8 (Theriot Av.)
   R–County Route 30/just after I-87 underpass
   R–continue south on County Route 10/between I-87 and Schroon River
   L–County Route 11/uphill
   Continue on back roads to Bolton Landing/downhill to Lake George
   R–Route 9N

3 Bolton Landing/food services; town beach
   R–just south of Bolton Landing/uphill
   L–Potter Hill Rd.
   R and then L–County Route 49/downhill to Lake George
   R–Route 9N

4 Diamond Point Beach
   R–County Route 35 at Diamond Point/uphill
   Bear R–US 9/after I-87 overpass

5 Warrensburg/bus service; food services
   Bear L–County Route 40

6 State Fish Hatchery
   Bear L–Route 28
   Return to the Glen House Hostel

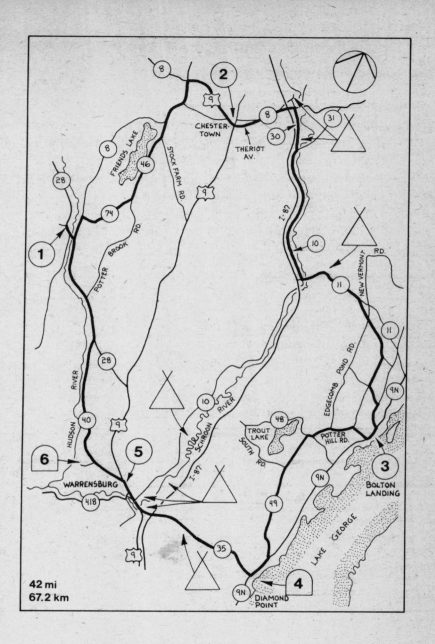

42 mi
67.2 km

Cranberry–Star Lake Tour (#18)

LAWRENCE COUNTY, NEW YORK

Length: *45 miles*

Terrain: *Rolling Hills*

Points of Interest: *Twin Falls of the South Branch Grasse River, Cranberry Lake, Benson Iron Mines, Star Lake*

Special Note: *this tour can be part of a weekend stay at the Star Lake Hostel or at a nearby campground*

1 Start at the Star Lake Hostel/Star Lake Campus, Star Lake, NY 13676; off Route 3 east of Watertown or west of Tupper Lake
   Go west on Route 3

2 Food Services
   R–Route 122/across Oswegatchie River east of Fine
   Continue north on Route 77 (Degrasse–Fine Rd.)
   R–Route 115 at Degrasse
   R–Tooley Pond Rd./one-half mile is unpaved near Route 3

3 Twin Falls/the South Branch Grasse River is part of New York's "Wild, Scenic, and Recreational River System"
   R (west)–Route 3

4 Food Services

5 Cranberry Lake Campsite

6 Wanakena/hiking trail to High Falls; swimming in Oswegatchie River; food services
   Continue west on Route 3

7 Benson Iron Mines/large open-pit iron mine
   Return to Star Lake Hostel

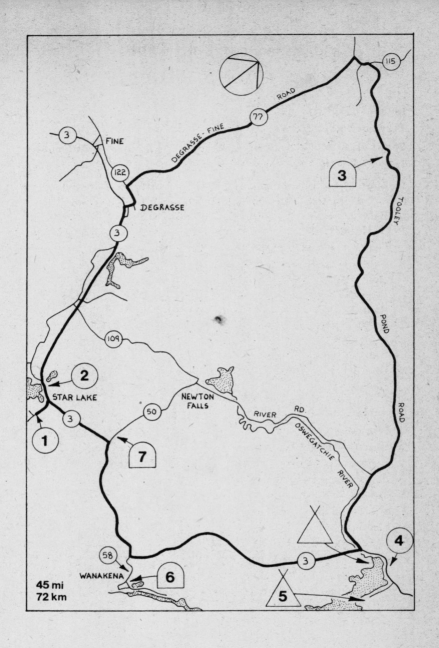

Riverhead Tour (#19)

SUFFOLK COUNTY, NEW YORK

Length: *65 miles*
Terrain: *Level*
Points of Interest: *eastern Long Island, Shelter Island, Automotive Museum in Southampton*

1 Start at free municipal parking lot in Riverhead, Long Island, at
    E. Main St. and Peconic Av./train service; food services
R–E. Main St.
R–Hubbard Av.
R–Edgar Rd. at T-intersection
R–Meetinghouse Creek Rd.
L–Peconic Bay Blvd.
L–Bay Av.
R–Main Rd. (Route 25)/through Mattituck
L–Mill Lane
R–Oregon Av.
R–Bridge Lane
L–North Rd. (Route 27)
L–Mill Rd.
R–Sound View Av.
Continue on Route 27
R–Albertson Dr.
Bear L–Cassidy Lane
L–Main Rd. (Route 25)/becomes Front St. and enters Greenport
R–3rd St. to ferry landing
Ferry to Shelter Island

2 Shelter Island/food services
Continue up Clinton Av.
Bear R–North Ferry Rd.
Continue onto Manwaring Rd.
R–Ram Island Rd.
Continue onto Ferry Rd. (Route 114) to ferry landing
Ferry to Sag Harbor
Continue on Main St. to Sag Harbor

3 Sag Harbor/food services
R–Brick Kiln Rd./road bears right

94

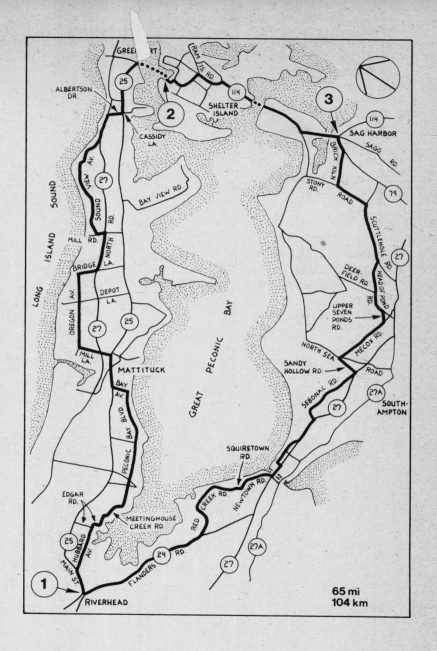

GREENPORT

IRAM IS. RD.

ALBERTSON DR.

25

②

114

SHELTER ISLAND

③

114

SAG HARBOR

SAGG RD.

CASSIDY LA.

BAY VIEW RD.

BRICK KILN

STONY RD.

ROAD

79

VIEW AV.

27

SOUND RD.

LONG ISLAND SOUND

MILL RD.

NORTH LA.

BRIDGE

OREGON AV.

DEPOT LA.

27

25

SCUTTLEHOLE RD.

HEAD OF POND RD.

27

DEER-FIELD RD.

UPPER SEVEN PONDS RD.

GREAT PECONIC BAY

MECOX RD.

NORTH SEA ROAD

MILL LA.

MATTITUCK

BAY AV.

PECONIC BAY BLVD.

SANDY HOLLOW RD.

SEBONAC RD.

27

27A

SOUTH-AMPTON

EDGAR RD.

MEETINGHOUSE CREEK RD.

SQUIRETOWN RD.

25

HUBBARD AV.

RED CREEK RD.

NEWTOWN RD.

24

FLANDERS RD.

27

27A

①

MAIN ST.

RIVERHEAD

65 mi
104 km

R–Huntington Path (or Scuttlehole Rd.)
R–Head of Pond Rd.
R–Upper Seven Ponds Rd.
R–Mecox Rd./through Hampton Park to North Sea Rd.
L–Sandy Hollow Rd.
R–Sebonac Rd./becomes New North Hwy. Rd. and leads into Shrubland Rd.
R–Sunrise Hwy. (Route 27)
Cross Shinnecock Canal
R–Newtown Rd.
L–Newtown Rd. at T-intersection
R–Squiretown Rd. at T-intersection/becomes Upper Red Creek Rd.
L–Lower Red Creek Rd.
R–Red Creek Rd.
R–Riverhead-Hampton Bays Rd. (Route 24)/becomes Flanders Rd.
Return to Riverhead

CHAPTER FIVE
Mid-Atlantic

New Jersey
Pennsylvania
Delaware
Maryland
Virginia

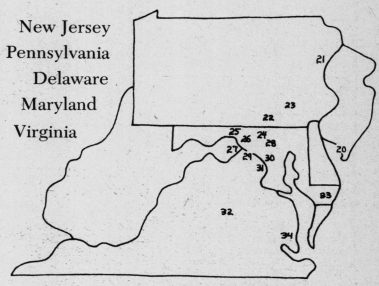

District of Columbia
West Virginia

Upper Cape May County (#20)

CAPE MAY COUNTY, NEW JERSEY

Length: *38 miles*
Terrain: *Level*
Points of Interest: *Great Cedar Swamp, Belleplain State Forest*

1 Start at Magnolia Lake on US 9 at Ocean View in southeast New
    Jersey
  Go south on US 9
  R–first road after Magnolia Lake
  L–South Dennis-Ocean View Rd.
  Bear R–Route 83 at South Dennis
  R–Route 47
  R–North Dennis-Marshallville Rd. (Route 557)
  L–first left turn
  Continue around west side of Lake Nummi

2 Belleplain State Forest
  L–Belleplain Rd.
  R–Belleplain Rd. at Belleplain
  R–Tuckahoe-County Line Rd.
  Continue onto Route 49
  R–before railroad tracks
  L–Mill Rd.-Reading Av./into Tuckahoe
  R–Route 50
  Bear L–Tuckahoe Rd.
  R–Tyler Rd.
  Continue onto Greenfield Rd.
  Rejoin Route 50
  R–US 9/watch traffic
  Return to Magnolia Lake

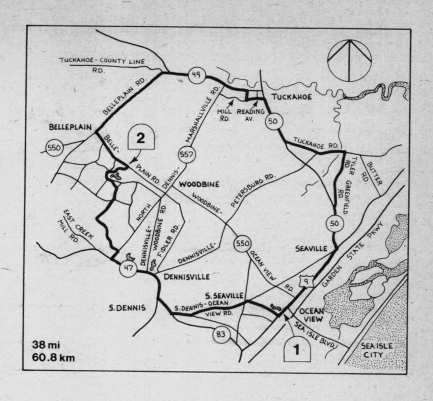

38 mi
60.8 km

Delaware Water Gap–Poconos Tour (#21)

MONROE AND PIKE COUNTIES, PENNSYLVANIA
WARREN AND SUSSEX COUNTIES, NEW JERSEY

Length: *135 miles*
Terrain: *Hilly*
Points of Interest: *Delaware River, Delaware Water Gap Natl. Recreation Area, Promised Land State Park, Pocono Mountains*

1. Start at Rising Waters Hostel/Box 223, Bushkill, PA 18324; northeast of Stroudsburg off US 209
   L–downhill from hostel

2. Bushkill/food services
   R–US 209/heavy traffic for two miles
   L–River Rd. at Shoemaker/to Delaware Water Gap

3. Delaware Water Gap Natl. Recreation Area
   Cross big bridge over Delaware River
   R–on road that goes off and curves back under I-80
   North on Old Mine Rd.
   Cross Route 739

4. Layton/food services
   Continue north on Old Mine Rd.

5. Old Mine Road Hostel/Box 172, Layton, NJ 07851
   Return to Route 739
   R–Route 739/across Delaware River
   L–to Blooming Grove

6. Blooming Grove/food services
   R–Route 402
   L–US 6
   L–Route 590 at Wilsonville/follow signs to Safari Campground

7. Safari Campground/food services; 717-226-3317
   Return to Wilsonville
   R–US 6
   R–Route 507
   Bear L–Route 390

8. Promised Land S.P./swimming
   R–first right turn after park with small church on right-hand corner
   Continue west on high ridge

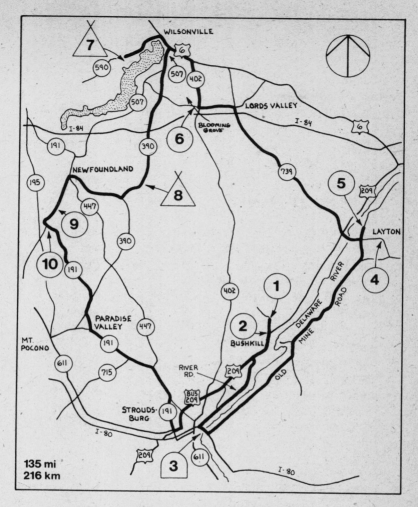

Keep forking left into Newfoundland/downhill
South on Route 191 at Newfoundland

9 South Sterling/food services

10 La Anna Hostel/Rt. 2, Box 1026, Cresco, PA 18326
Continue south on Route 191/five-mile uphill followed by downhill
L–Business US 209 at East Stroudsburg
Continue on US 209/heavy traffic
Return to Rising Waters Hostel

Gettysburg Battlefield Tour (#22)

ADAMS COUNTY, PENNSYLVANIA

Length: *15 miles*

Terrain: *Rolling Hills*

Points of Interest: *Gettysburg National Military Park, including Little Round Top, Seminary Ridge, and Culp's Hill*

Special Note: *for a good map of the battlefield, write Gettysburg National Military Park, Gettysburg, PA 17325*

1 Start at the Visitor Center just off Route 134 south of Gettysburg/bus service; motels; food services

   R—Route 134 (Taneytown Rd.)

   R—at first road

   L—Hancock Av./pass the Cyclorama

2 High Water Mark/Pickett's Charge was halted here on July 3, 1863, bringing the battle to a close

3 Little Round Top/on July 2, 1863, Longstreet's charge through The Peach Orchard and The Cornfield west of here foundered on the slopes of this hill

   Continue over Big Round Top

   Cross Business US 15

   Straight on Confederate Av.

4 Seminary Ridge/much of the Confederate army was drawn up along this ridge

   L—Fairfield Rd. (Route 116)

   R—Reynolds Av.

   L—Buford Av.

   Cross Mummasburg Rd.

5 Eternal Peace Memorial

   Recross Mummasburg Rd.

   Bear L around Oak Ridge

   R—Mummasburg Rd.

   L—Howard Av.

   R—Harrisburg Rd. (Business US 15)

   L—Stratton St.

   L—E. Middle St.

   R—E. Confederate Av./continue to Culp's Hill

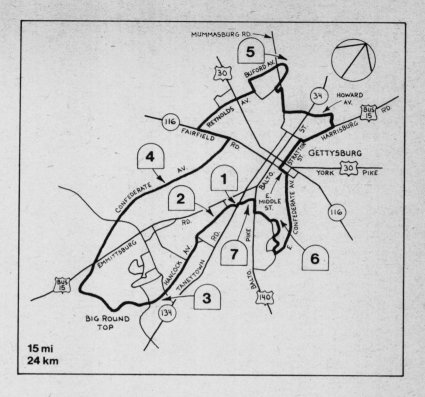

6 Culp's Hill/Union defenders here repelled Ewell's Confederates
      late on July 2, 1863
    R–Baltimore Pike (US 140)
    L–through National Cemetery

7 National Cemetery/here President Lincoln delivered his Gettys-
      burg Address
    Return to Visitor Center

Pennsylvania Dutch Tour (#23)

LANCASTER COUNTY, PENNSYLVANIA

Length: *42.5 miles*
Terrain: *Rolling Hills*
Points of Interest: *rolling Amish farmland, Swiss cheese factory, gristmill, chair factory, several "hex" barns, horses and buggies, great food*

1 Start at Bowmansville Hostel/Box 117, Bowmansville, PA 17507; in center of town at jct. of Route 625 and Maple Grove Rd.; food services
Go west on Maple Grove Rd.
L—Route 897 at Fivepointville
L—Main St.

2 Terre Hill/food services
R—Lancaster Av.

3 Martindale/food services
L—Grist Mill Rd. at Martindale
Cross US 322
Continue on Linden Grove Rd.
L—Shirk Rd. at road sign: New Holland 3 miles
Cross Route 23
Bear R—S. Shirk Rd./Nolt Rd. Goes off to left
L—Zeltenreich Rd.
R—Centerville Rd.

4 Swiss Cheese Factory
Return to Zeltenreich Rd. and turn left
L—Musser School Rd.
R—Groffdale Rd.
Continue ½ mile past E. Eby Rd. on Groffdale Rd.

5 Hayloft Candles/homemade ice cream, gift and candle shop, closed Sunday
Return to E. Eby Rd. and turn R
L—Mascot Rd.

6 Gristmill
L—Newport Rd. (Route 772)
R—Hess Rd. (Route 772)

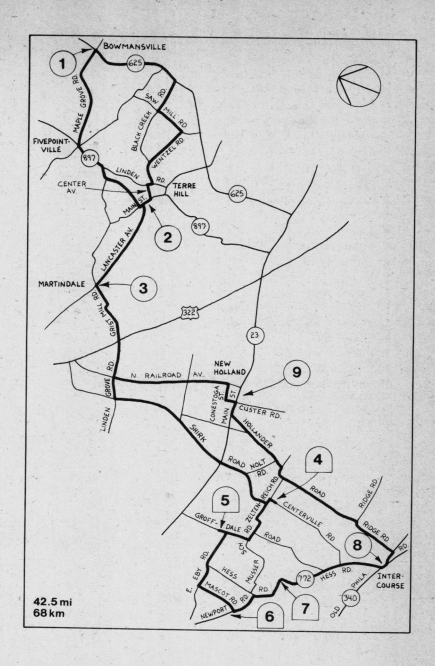

BOWMANSVILLE

1

625

MAPLE GROVE RD.

SAW MILL RD.

BLACK CREEK

WENTZEL RD.

FIVEPOINT-
VILLE

897

LINDEN RD.

CENTER AV.

MAIN ST.

TERRE HILL

625

897

2

LANCASTER AV.

MARTINDALE

3

GRIST MILL RD.

322

23

GROVE RD.

N. RAILROAD AV.

NEW HOLLAND

9

LINDEN

CONESTOGA ST.

MAIN ST.

CUSTER RD.

SHIRK

HOLLANDER

ROAD

NOLT RD.

4

ROAD

REICH RD.

RIDGE RD.

5

ZELTENREICH RD.

CENTERVILLE RD.

RIDGE RD.

GROFF-DALE RD.

ROAD

8

RD.

E. EBY RD.

HESS RD.

KOCH RD.

MUSSER RD.

772

HESS RD.

OLD PHILA. RD.

INTER-
COURSE

MASCOT RD.

RD.

340

NEWPORT

6

7

42.5 mi
68 km

7 Eversole's Chair Shop

8 Intercourse/food services
L–Old Philadelphia Rd. (Route 340)
Bear L at fork (Route 340)
L–Ridge Rd. at Traveler's Rest Motel
R–Ridge Rd./hex barn on left
L–Hollander Rd. to New Holland
R–Main St.

9 New Holland/food services
L–Custer Rd. at traffic light
R–Conestoga St./about 3 blocks from Custer Rd.
L–North Railroad Av.
R–Linden Grove Rd. at road sign: Martindale 2 mile:
Continue on Grist Mill Rd.
R–Lancaster Av.
R–Main St. at Terre Hill
L–Center Av.
R–Linden Rd./continue for about 200 feet
L–Wentzel Rd./may be unsigned
L–Saw Mill Rd.
R–Black Creek Rd.
L–Route 625
Return to Bowmansville Hostel

Catoctin Climber (#24)

FREDERICK COUNTY, MARYLAND

Length: 55 *miles*

Terrain: *Rolling Hills to Very Hilly*

Points of Interest: *Catoctin Furnace, Cunningham Falls State Park, Catoctin Mountain National Park, Main's Ice Cream Shop*

1   Start at Prospect Plaza Shopping Center just off US 15 on S. Jefferson St. (US 340) in Frederick/bus service; motels; food services; bike shops
    L—S. Jefferson St./city traffic
    R—W. South St. (Route 144)
    L—S. Market St. (Route 355)
    L—9th St.
    R—Motter Av.
    Straight on Opossumtown Pike
    Bear R—Opossumtown Pike at Ford Rd./unsigned
    L—Opossumtown Pike at Masser Rd./unsigned
    R—Bethel Rd.
    R—Fish Hatchery Rd.
    L—Route 806 in Lewistown

2   Lewistown/food services

3   Catoctin Furnace/old ironworks site

4   Cunningham Falls State Park
    L—Church St. in Thurmont

5   Thurmont/food services
    Straight on Route 550 (Sabillasville Rd.)/long uphill
    L—Foxville-Deerfield Rd. at stop sign

6   Catoctin Mountain Park/Owens Creek Campground
    Cross Route 77
    Straight on Stottlemeyer Rd.
    L—Smithsburg Rd. (Route 153) in Wolfsville
    Bear R—Harp Hill Rd./steep hills
    Cross bridge and enter Ellerton
    Bear L—Harmony-Ellerton Rd./hills
    L—Middletown-Myersville Rd.

7   Middletown/food services: Main's Ice Cream Shop

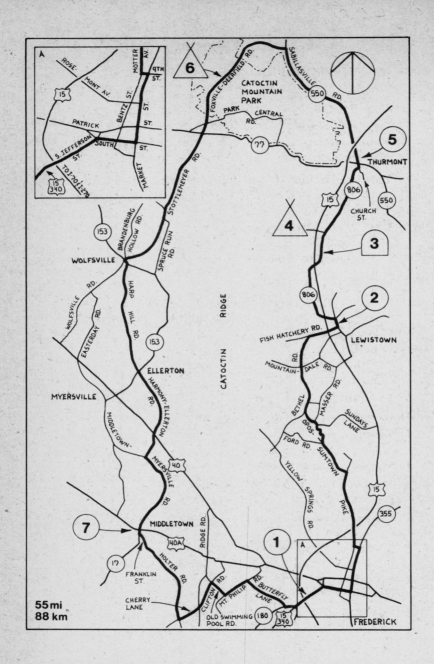

A
ROSE. AV.
MONT AV.
MOTTER AV.
9TH ST.
15
BENTZ ST.
STS.
PATRICK
S. JEFFERSON ST.
SOUTH ST.
MARKET ST.
TO 15/340

6

CATOCTIN
MOUNTAIN
PARK
FOXVILLE-DEERFIELD RD.
SABILLASVILLE RD.
550
PARK
RD.
CENTRAL
RD.
77

STOTTLEMEYER RD.

5
THURMONT
806
15
550
CHURCH
ST.

4

3

153
BRANDENBURG
HOLLOW RD.
WOLFSVILLE
SPRUCE RUN RD.

806

2
LEWISTOWN
FISH HATCHERY RD.

WOLFSVILLE RD.
HARP HILL RD.
153
EASTERDAY RD.

MOUNTAIN-DALE RD.

MASSER RD.
BETHEL RD.
SUNDAYS
LANE

ELLERTON

MYERSVILLE
HARMONY-ELLERTON RD.
MIDDLETOWN-
MYERSVILLE RD.

CATOCTIN   RIDGE

OPOS.
FORD RD.
SLIMTOWN
YELLOW
SPRINGS
RD.

40

15
355

7
MIDDLETOWN
40A
RIDGE RD.
17
FRANKLIN
ST.
HOLTER RD.

1
A

CHERRY
LANE
CLIFTON RD.
MT. PHILIP RD.
BUTTERFLY
LANE
OLD SWIMMING
POOL RD.
180
15
340
FREDERICK

55 mi
88 km

108

Straight on Route 17
L–Franklin St.
Straight on Holter Rd.
L–Cherry Lane/uphill
Straight on Clifton Rd./steep downhill
R–Old Swimming Pool Rd. at bottom of hill
L–Mt. Phillip Rd.
R–Butterfly Lane
L–Route 180
R–onto US 340 north
Return to Prospect Plaza

Falling Waters–Fort Frederick Tour (#25)

WASHINGTON COUNTY, MARYLAND

Length: *37.5 miles*

Terrain: *Level to Rolling Hills*

Points of Interest: *Chesapeake & Ohio Canal National Historical Park, Fort Frederick State Park*

1   Start at Falling Waters Hostel/RR 1, Box 238-B, Williamsport, MD 21795; at end of Falling Waters Rd., six miles south of Williamsport, Maryland
Go L down dirt road in front of hostel
R–C & O Canal towpath/packed dirt surface for next 20 miles

2   Williamsport/old canal town; food services

3   Conococheague Aqueduct/the canal crosses Conococheague Creek

4   Dam No. 5/the dam supplied water to the old canal

5   Four Locks/the canal shortcuts across Prathers Neck here
R–on unmarked dirt road after Milepost 112/at downstream end of lake .
Continue up hill

6   Fort Frederick State Park/built during French & Indian War
Continue on paved road
R–Route 56 (Big Pool Rd.)
R–Route 68
Continue through Williamsport on Conococheague St. (Route 68)
R–Route 63 after I-81 underpass
R–Falling Waters Rd.
Continue straight down dirt road to Falling Waters Hostel

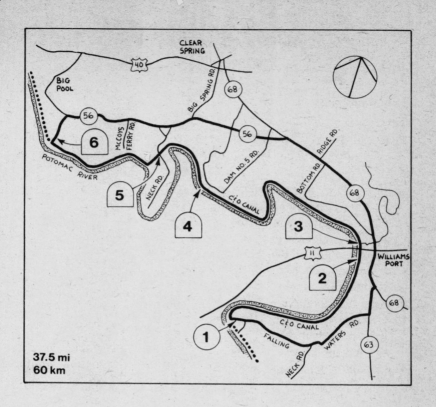

37.5 mi
60 km

111

Antietam Campaign (#26)

FREDERICK AND WASHINGTON COUNTIES, MARYLAND

Length: *40 miles*
Terrain: *Level to Hilly*
Points of Interest: *South Mountain and Gathland State Park, Antietam National Battlefield Site, Chesapeake & Ohio Canal NHP*

1 Start at the Kiwanis Hostel/Rt. 2, Box 304, Knoxville, MD 21758; 16 miles west of Frederick off US 340; food services
   Go R (uphill) on Sandy Hook Rd.
   R–Route 180/unsigned
   Bear L–up to US 340
   R–US 340/stay on shoulder and watch traffic
   R–Route 180

2 Knoxville/food services
   Continue on Route 180/uphill
   L–Catholic Church Rd.
   L–Gapland Rd./steep uphill after Burkittsville; watch for dogs!

3 Crampton Gap and Gathland State Park/the Battle of South Mountain here on Sept. 14, 1862, was the first engagement of the Antietam Campaign
   R–Townsend Rd./downhill
   R–Route 67
   L–Trego Rd.
   Straight on Porterstown Rd.
   L–Burnside Bridge Rd.
   Straight on Route 65 at Main St. in Sharpsburg

4 Sharpsburg/food services
   R–Antietam National Battlefield Site

5 Battlefield Visitor Center/get a park map; the Battle of Antietam or Sharpsburg was fought on Sept. 17, 1862
   Follow the battlefield tour/our tour varies slightly from the Park Service tour

6 The Cornfield/morning phase of the battle
7 Sunken Road/midday phase of the battle
8 Burnside Bridge/afternoon phase of the battle
   L–Harpers Ferry Rd./leave battlefield tour

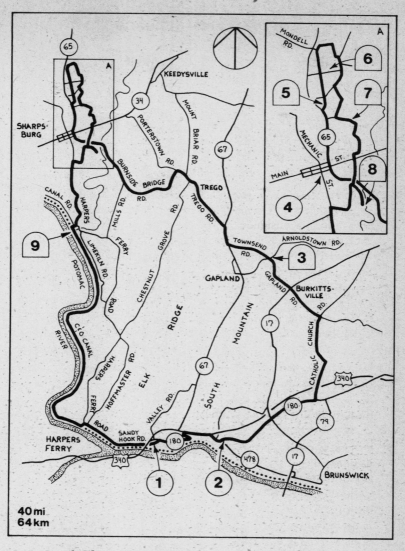

R–Canal Rd. at C & O Canal sign
L–on C & O Canal towpath/packed dirt surface for next 8 miles

9 Antietam Aqueduct/the canal crosses Antietam Creek
L–leave canal towpath at Lock 34
R–onto Harpers Ferry Rd.
Return to Kiwanis Hostel/uphill from Sandy Hook

Harpers Ferry–Lower Shenandoah Valley Tour (#27)

Length: *32 miles one way*
Terrain: *Rolling Hills*
Points of Interest: *Harpers Ferry National Historical Park, Shenandoah River, Burwell-Morgan Gristmill*

1 Start at Harpers Ferry NHP off US 340, 20 miles west of Frederick, Maryland/food services; restored 19th-century community
   Go R on Shenandoah St. from parking area
   L–High St./steep uphill
   Continue on Washington St.
   Bear L then R–US 340
   L–Bloomery Rd./opposite Bakerton Rd. at bottom of hill
   R–Route 9/watch traffic
   L–Kabletown Rd.

2 Kabletown/food services
   L–to Virginia Route 608/unsigned
   Enter Virginia
   L–continue on Route 608
   R–State Route 7/watch traffic
   L–Business Route 7

3 Berryville/food services
   L–Route 613
   L–Continue on Route 613
   R–Route 618
   R–Route 617
   L–State Route 255

4 Millwood/food services

5 Burwell-Morgan Gristmill/the site is being restored by the Clarke County Historical Society

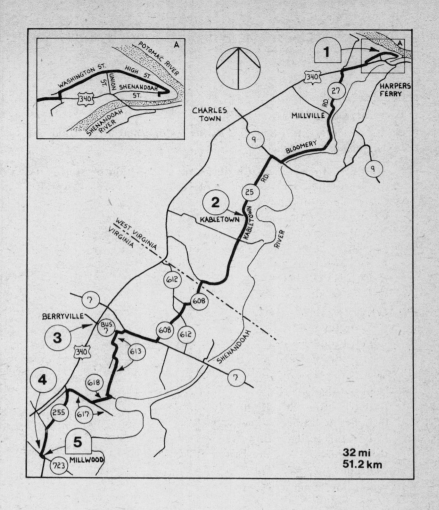

32 mi
51.2 km

Frederick County Covered Bridge Tour (#28)

FREDERICK COUNTY, MARYLAND

Length: *42 miles*

Terrain: *Rolling Hills*

Points of Interest: *rural farmlands, Monocacy River, covered bridge*

1 Start at Staley Park in Frederick at intersection of Motter Av. and 9th St./bus service; motels; food services; bike shops
   Go north on Motter Av.
   Continue on Opossumtown Pike
   Bear R–Opossumtown Pike at Ford Rd./unsigned
   L–Opossumtown Pike at Masser Rd./unsigned
   R–Bethel Rd.
   R–Fish Hatchery Rd.
   R–Route 806

2 Lewistown/food services
   L–Lewistown Rd.
   L–Old Frederick Rd.
   Bear L–Route 550
   Bear R–Old Frederick Rd.

3 Covered Bridge
   R–Rocky Ridge Rd. (Route 77)
   R–Longs Mill Rd.
   L–Le Gore Bridge Rd.
   R–Continue on Le Gore Bridge Rd./steep hill
   Continue on Route 194

4 Woodsboro/food services
   L–Route 550
   R–Hoffman-Seachrist Rd. at quarry
   Continue on Daysville Rd.
   L–Water Street Rd. Cross Route 26
   Continue straight on Old Annapolis Rd.
   R–McKaig Rd./several hills follow
   R–Gas House Pike/one steep hill
   Continue on E. Church St.
   Bear R–E. 2nd St.
   R–Market St./city traffic

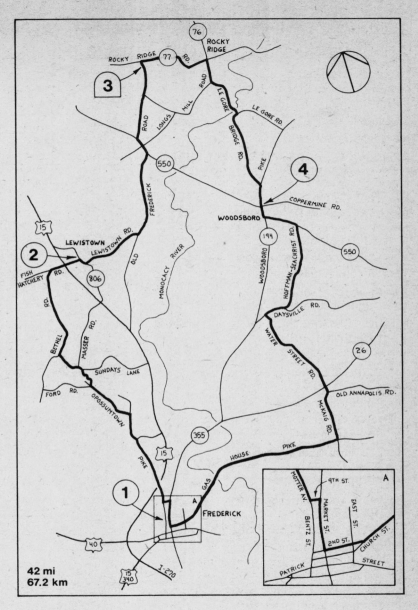

L–9th St.
Return to Staley Park

White's Ferry Crossing (#29)

FREDERICK AND MONTGOMERY COUNTIES, MARYLAND
LOUDOUN COUNTY, VIRGINIA

Length: *38 miles*
Terrain: *Rolling Hills*
Points of Interest: *Point of Rocks Railroad Station, White's Ferry, Potomac River*

1   Start at Point of Rocks Railroad Station just off Route 28 near jct.
    US 15 in Point of Rocks, Maryland/the station is on National
    Register of Historic Places; food services nearby
    Go east on Route 28
    L—continue on Route 28 at Route 85

2   Dickerson/food services

3   Monocacy Aqueduct/the C & O Canal crosses the Monocacy
    River
    Bear R—Martinsburg Rd./narrow pavement
    L—Wasche Rd.
    R—White's Ferry Rd.

4   White's Ferry/only continuously operating ferry across Potomac;
    fee for bicycles; food services
    Continue on Route 655
    L—US 15/watch for heavy traffic
    Straight on Bus. US 15

5   Leesburg/food services
    R—W. Cornwall St.
    L—Liberty St.
    Cross Market St. (Route 7)
    R—Loudoun St.
    L—Dry Mill Rd./rough road in spots
    Continue over Route 7
    Straight on Route 9/watch traffic
    R—Route 662
    Straight on Route 665 in Waterford/several hills
    L—Route 663
    Straight on Route 668

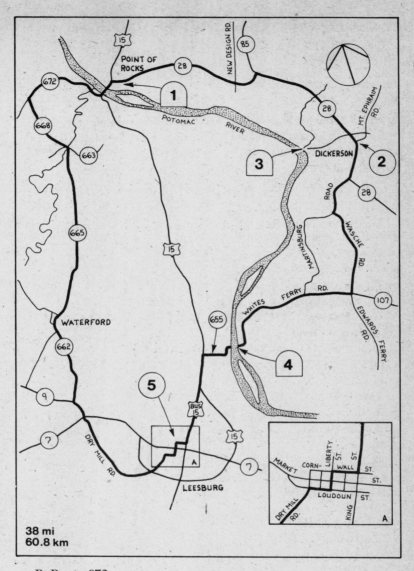

R–Route 672
L–US 15/cross Potomac River; watch for heavy traffic
R–Route 28
Return to Point of Rocks Railroad Station

Potomac Parks and the Mall (#30)

DISTRICT OF COLUMBIA

Length: *10 miles*

Terrain: *Level*

Points of Interest: *Washington Monument, Lincoln Memorial, West Potomac Park, Jefferson Memorial, East Potomac Park, the Mall, the Capitol, and the White House.*

Special Note: *use extreme care when cycling along or across city streets. Lock your bike if you leave it.*

1 Start at the Washington Monument
   Go west on sidewalk toward Lincoln Memorial
   Cross 17th St., NW
   Continue west on sidewalk on left side of Constitution Av.
   L—on sidewalk on left side of Bacon Dr.

2 Lincoln Memorial
   Continue clockwise around Lincoln Memorial
   L—on first street not blocked off to traffic/walk bike to right-hand
      side of road
   Continue into West Potomac Park (Ohio Dr.)
   Bear R—cross Tidal Basin Bridge
   L—to Jefferson Memorial

3 Jefferson Memorial
   Return toward Tidal Basin Bridge and bear L (Ohio Dr.)
   Continue around East Potomac Park

4 Hains Point
   R—on road after underpass
   L—at traffic light/busy intersection
   R—15th St., NW
   Cross Independence Av.
   R—at next road
   Continue on Jefferson Dr. onto the Mall

5 The Mall/Smithsonian Institution museums include the Arts & Industries Building, the Hirshhorn Museum, the Air & Space Museum, the National Gallery of Art, the Museum of Natural History, and the Museum of History & Technology
   L—3rd St., NW

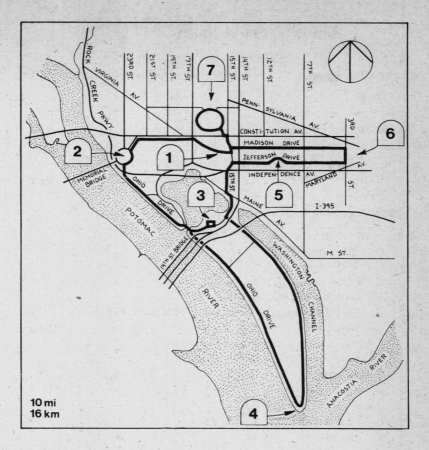

6 The Capitol
  L–Madison Dr.
  R–15th St., NW
  At Constitution Av., walk bike across to opposite corner
  Cycle clockwise around the Ellipse
7 The White House
  Leave the Ellipse, recross Constitution Av., return to the
  Washington Monument

Mount Vernon Bike Trail (#31)

DISTRICT OF COLUMBIA
ARLINGTON COUNTY, ALEXANDRIA CITY, AND FAIRFAX COUNTY, VIRGINIA

Length: *15.7 miles one way*

Terrain: *Level*

Points of Interest: *Lincoln Memorial, Potomac River, National Airport, Old Town Alexandria, Fort Hunt Park, and Mount Vernon.*

Special Note: *this entire bike trail is marked with signs.*

1   Start at Lincoln Memorial at the west end of the Mall in Washington, DC
Circle clockwise around the Lincoln Memorial
Walk bike across to left sidewalk of Memorial Bridge
Continue across Memorial Bridge
Bear L–paved bike trail/cross G.W. Memorial Pkwy. ramps with care
Continue south along Potomac River
Continue to opposite corner of parking lot at Gravelly Point
Cross National Airport access roads with care
Continue past Sailing Marina/steep hill follows
Continue on sidewalk along E. Abingdon St.
L–on bike path after railroad tracks
L–Pendleton St.
R–Union St.

2   Alexandria waterfront and Old Town Alexandria
R–Franklin St.
L–Lee St.
R–Jefferson St.
L–Royal St.
Continue under Beltway and past apartment bldg./obey trail signs
L–bike path
Continue past Belle Haven/very narrow trail in sections; gravel surface; trail crosses Dyke Marsh on boardwalk
Continue onto Northdown Rd.
R–Alexandria Av.

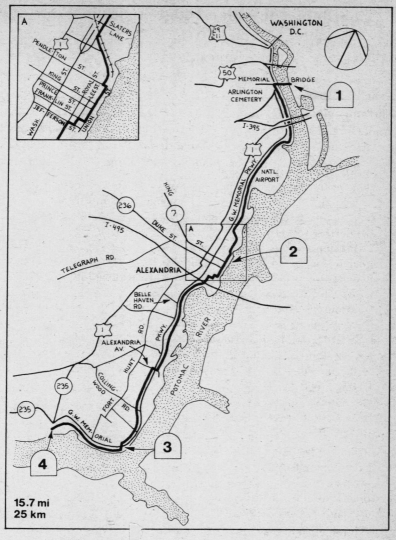

L–bike path

Bear L–under G.W. Memorial Pkwy. at Fort Hunt Park

3 Fort Hunt Park

Arrive at Mt. Vernon

4 Mt. Vernon/home of George Washington; entrance fee; food
services

Charlottesville–Blue Ridge Foothills Tour
(#32)

ALBEMARLE COUNTY, VIRGINIA

Length: *52 miles*
Terrain: *Rolling Hills*
Points of Interest: *University of Virginia, views of the Blue Ridge Mountains, horse farms, Rivanna Reservoir*
Special Note: *get an early start to avoid city traffic.*

1 Start at the Rotunda of the Univ. of Virginia, University Av. at Rugby Rd. in Charlottesville/plane, bus, and train service; motels; food services; bike shops
  Go north on Rugby Rd.
  L–Preston Av.
  Bear R–Rugby Rd./*not* on Rugby Av.
  Bear L–Rugby Rd. extended/steep, narrow downhill
  Cross US 250
  Continue on Hydraulic Rd.
  Cross US 29
  Stay on Hydraulic Rd. (Route 743)
  Bear L–Route 743/downhill
  L–Route 676
  R–Route 660
  L–Route 743
  Bear L–Route 663 at Earlysville
  Bear L–Route 664
  Bear L–Route 665
2 Free Union/food services
  R–Route 601
  Bear L–Route 810 at Boonesville
  L–Route 614 at Whitehall
3 Whitehall/food services
  Continue straight on Routes 676 and 601
  R–Route 601 (Garth Rd.)
  Bear L–Route 754/over US 29-250 Bypass
  Bear L–US 250 (Ivy Rd.)/watch traffic

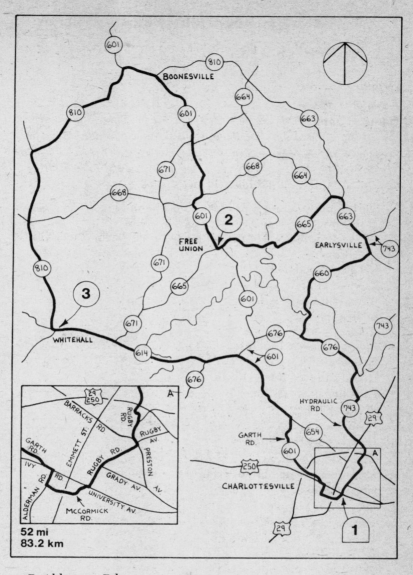

R–Alderman Rd.
L–McCormick Rd./through University of Virginia Grounds
Return to Rotunda

Viewtrail 100 (#33)

WORCESTER COUNTY, MARYLAND

Length: *100 miles*

Terrain: *Level*

Points of Interest: *Pocomoke River and Pocomoke State Forest, Milburn Landing State Park, cypress swamp, wildlife.*

Special Note: *this entire trail is signed; for a trail brochure, write Worcester County Extension Service, County Service Bldg., 107 E. Market St., Snow Hill, MD 21863.*

1   Start in Berlin south of US 50 off US 113 on Maryland's Eastern
       Shore/bus service; motels; food services
     Go west on Route 374 (Broad St. becomes Berlin-Libertytown
       Rd.)
     L—Patey Woods Rd.
     R—Ninepin Branch Rd.
     R—Whiton Crossing Rd.
     L—Shockley Rd.
     R—Laws Rd.
     L—Mt. Olive Church Rd.
     L—Route 12
     R—Old Furnace Rd.
     L—Millville Creek Rd.
     R—Scotty Rd.
     R and then L—at Corbin
     Fork L/Oak Hall Rd. forks R
     Bear R—Route 364 (Dividing Creek Rd.)/turn L for camping

2   Milburn Landing State Park/primitive camping
     Cross US 13
     Bear L into Pocomoke City

3   Pocomoke City/food services
     R—Route 371 (Cedarhall Rd.)
     L—Dunn Swamp Rd.
     L—Tulls Corner Rd.
     R then L—Bunting Rd./cross US 13
     Bear L twice—Payne Rd.
     R—Brantley Rd.
     Straight on Sheephouse Rd.

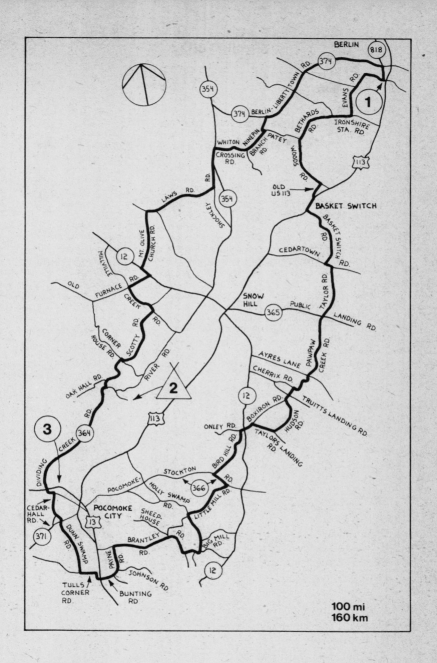

L–Big Mill Rd. at Welbourne
Bear L–next road
R–Little Mill Rd.
L–Route 366
R–Bird Hill Rd.
R–cross Route 12 onto Boxiron Rd.
R–Taylors Landing Rd.
L–Hudson Rd.
R–Boxiron Rd.
R then L–across Truitts Landing Rd.
R–at Boxiron
Continue north on Pawpaw Creek Rd.
Straight on Taylor Rd.
L–Cedartown Rd.
R–Basket Switch Rd.
R–US 113 at Basket Switch/watch traffic
Fork L on Old US 113
L–Patey Woods Rd.
Bear R–Bethards Rd.
Straight on Ironshire Station Rd.
L–Evans Rd.
L–Route 818
Return to Berlin

Virginia Tidewater Tour (#34)

JAMES CITY, YORK, GLOUCESTER, MIDDLESEX, KING AND QUEEN, KING WILLIAM, HANOVER, CHARLES CITY, AND NEW KENT COUNTIES, VIRGINIA

Length: *170 miles*

Terrain: *Level*

Points of Interest: *Colonial Williamsburg, Jamestown, Yorktown, Colonial Parkway, rural tidewater country*

Special Note: *for brochure "Biking Through Virginia's Historic Triangle," write Bicycling Coordinator, Virginia Dept. of Transportation, 1401 E. Broad St., Richmond, VA 23219*

1 Start at Colonial Williamsburg Information Center between Route 132 and Colonial Pkwy. just north of town/train and bus service; motels; food services; bike shops; restored Colonial Capitol of Virginia

Go L (east) onto Colonial Pkwy.

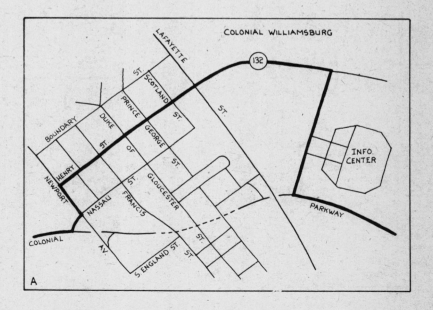

2 Yorktown Battlefield
Go north on US 17/cross York River; heavy traffic
R–just after bridge on Route 1204
L–Route 1208
Rejoin US 17
Bear L–Route 1216/through Hayes
Rejoin US 17

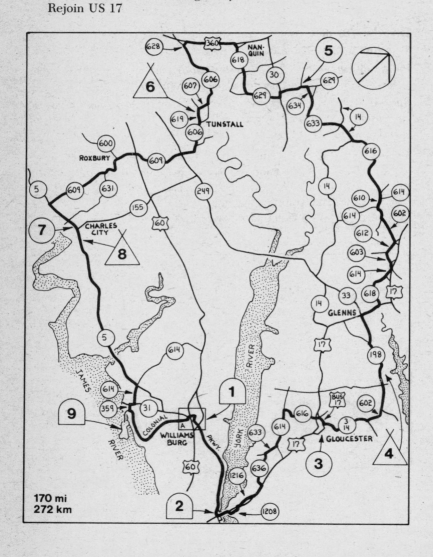

170 mi
272 km

L–Route 636
Bear R–Route 633
L–Route 614
R–Route 616
R–Business US 17/at Gloucester

3 Gloucester/food services
L–State Routes 3 & 14
L–Route 602
L–State Route 198

4 Cypress Shores KOA
R–US 17
L–Route 618
L–Route 614
Rejoin US 17
Bear L–Route 603 at Warner
R–Route 612
L–Route 602
Bear R–Route 610
Fork L–Route 616 after Dragonville
R–State Route 14
Straight on Route 633
Fork L–Route 634
L–Route 629

5 Walkerton/food services
L then R–across State Route 30 to Route 629
R–Route 618
L–US 360/heavy traffic
L–Route 628/gravel road
L–Route 606
R–Route 607
L–Route 619

6 Woodborn KOA
R–Route 606
R–Route 609
L–State Route 5

7 Charles City/food services

8 New Hope Campground
R–Route 614
R then L–across State Route 31

9 Jamestown
East on Colonial Pkwy
Exit L to Colonial Williamsburg before tunnel
L–Newport Av.
R–Henry St.
Continue on Route 132 across Lafayette St.
Return to Information Center

CHAPTER SIX
Southeast

North Carolina
Tennessee
Alabama
Mississippi
Florida

Smoky Mountains Tour (#35)

GRAHAM AND SWAIN COUNTIES, NORTH CAROLINA
BLOUNT AND SEVIER COUNTIES, TENNESSEE

Length: *199.5 miles*

Terrain: *Hilly to Very Hilly*

Points of Interest: *Smoky Mountains National Park, Calderwood and Fontana Dams, Cherokee Indian Reservation*

Special Notes: *this tour is best taken in late May, June, or September when tourist traffic is light; for more information write Great Smoky Mountains National Park, Gatlinburg, TN 37738.*

1 Start at the Visitor Center & Park Headquarters near Gatlinburg

2 Gatlinburg/bus service; motels; food services
  Go west on Little River Rd. (Route 73)

3 Elkmont Campground
  Continue on Laurel Branch Rd./uphill to Cades Cove

4 Cades Cove Campground

5 Cades Cove/an 11-mile loop road passes open fields, poineer homesteads and little frame churches
  Return to Route 73
  L–Route 73 to Townsend

6 Townsend/motels; food services
  L–Foothills Pkwy.

7 Look Rock Campground
  L–US 129/long uphill to Deals Gap

8 Calderwood Dam

9 Deals Gap (el. 1,957 ft.)
  L–Route 28

10 Fontana Village/motels; food services

11 Fontana Dam

12 Cable Cove Campground/May 27–Sept. 5 only
  R–to Cheoah
  L–US 129/uphill over Snowbird Mtns.

13 Topton/food services
  L–US 19

14 Brookside Park Campground/Box 93, Topton, NC 28781; May

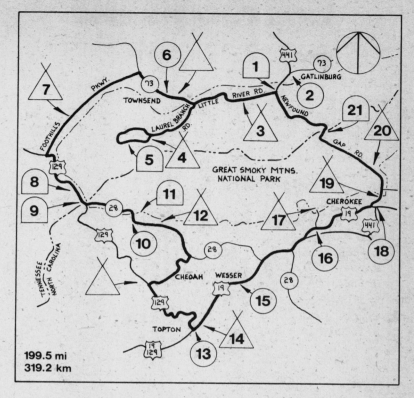

15–Sept. 15 only

15 Nantahala Outdoor Center/hostel & motel; food services; raft trips; canoe rentals; Star Route, Box 68, Bryson City, NC 28713

16 Bryson City/food services

17 Deep Creek Campground/2.5 miles off US 19

18 Cherokee/bus service; motels; food services
L–US 441 to Great Smoky Mtns. National Park

19 Piney Grove Campgrounds/Big Cove Rd., Cherokee, NC 28719

20 Smokemont Campground
Continue on Newfound Gap Road/long uphill climb

21 Newfound Gap (el. 5,048 ft.)
Continue on Newfound Gap Rd/long downhill with 2 short tunnels
Return to Visitor Center

Choctawhatchee Bay Loop (#36)

WALTON AND OKALOOSA COUNTIES, FLORIDA

Length: *79 miles*

Terrain: *Level*

Points of Interest: *Choctawhatchee Bay, Gulf of Mexico, John C. Beasley State Park, Rocky Bayou State Park*

1 Start at Ft. Walton Beach on US 98 east of Pensacola/food services

  Go north on Route 85 to Valparaiso

  R–Route 20

2 Rocky Bayou State Park

  Bear R–US 331

  L–US 98

  R–Route 283

  R–Route 30A

  L–US 98

3 John C. Beasley State Park

  Return to Ft. Walton Beach

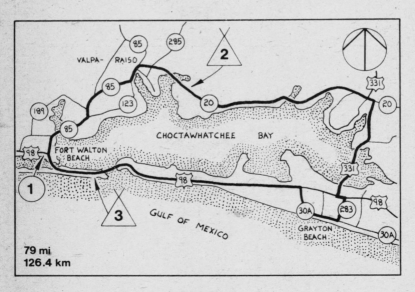

79 mi
126.4 km

Fort Morgan–Gulf of Mexico Tour (#37)

ESCAMBIA COUNTY, FLORIDA
BALDWIN COUNTY, ALABAMA

Length: *60 miles one way*
Terrain: *Level*
Points of Interest: *Gulf of Mexico, Gulf State Park, Fort Morgan*
Special Note: *winds can be very strong on this tour.*

1 Start in Pensacola/bus service; motels; food services
Go west on Bus. US 98 (Garden St.)
L–Pace Blvd. (Route 292)
Continue west on Barrancas Av. (Route 292)
Continue west on Route 292
Continue on Route 182 into Alabama
Bear R–to Gulf State Park

2 Gulf State Park
Cross Route 59
Continue west on Route 180

3 Fort Morgan

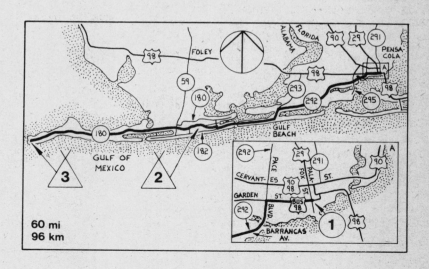

60 mi
96 km

Vicksburg to Mobile (#38)

WARREN, HINDS, CLAIBORNE, COPIAH, LINCOLN,
LAWRENCE, WALTHALL, MARION, LAMAR, FORREST,
STONE, GEORGE, AND JACKSON COUNTIES,
MISSISSIPPI
MOBILE COUNTY, ALABAMA

Length: *270 miles*
Terrain: *Rolling Hills*
Points of Interest: *Vicksburg Military Park, US Army Waterways
Experiment Station, Natchez Trace, rural Mississippi, Mobile.*

1 Start in Vicksburg off I-20 along the Mississippi River/bus
    service; motels; food services; there is a hilly 16-mile route
    through Vicksburg Military Park
    Go east on US 80
    R (south)–Route 27/pass US Army Waterways Experiment Sta-
    tion
    R (south)–Natchez Trace/historic North-South transportation
    route; for information write Natchez Trace Parkway, Rural
    Route 1, NT-143, Tupelo, MS 38801

2 Rocky Springs Campground
    Pedal through maintenance garage grounds at Port Gibson to
    Route 547
    East on Route 547

3 Pattison/food services
    L–Route 28
    R–unnumbered local road to Peelsville & Redstar
    L–Route 550

4 Brookhaven/motels; food services; bike shop
    East on US 84
    Bear R–unnumbered local road
    R–Route 27
    L–Route 586/continue to Columbia

5 Columbia/food services
    R (south)–Route 13
    R–US 49
    L–Route 26
    R–unnumbered local road

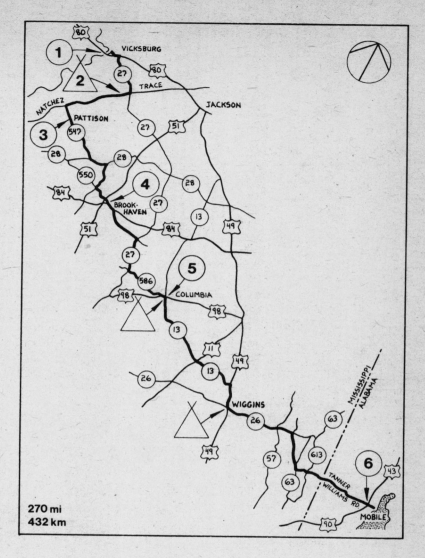

Continue south on Route 63

L–Tanner Williams (or Old Shell) Rd. to Tanner Williams, Alabama/becomes Route 10

Continue east on Route 10 into Mobile

6 Mobile/bus service; motels; food services; Bellingrath Gardens; Gulf of Mexico

CHAPTER SEVEN
Midwest & Great Lakes

Michigan
Ohio
Indiana
Illinois
Kentucky

Orchard Beach–Manistee Forest Tour (#39)

MANISTEE, WEXFORD, LAKE, AND MASON COUNTIES, MICHIGAN

Length: *100 miles*

Terrain: *Hilly*

Points of Interest: *Orchard Beach State Park, Manistee Forest, Manistee River, Manistee fishing docks*

1   Start at Orchard Beach State Park, north of Manistee on Lake Michigan, 119 miles north of Grand Rapids
    Go east on Kott Rd.
    L then R–Dontz Rd.
    L–Bar Lake Rd.
    R–Schoedel
    R–US 31
    L–Coates Hwy.
    R–High Bridge Rd.

2   Brethren/food services
    L–still Coates Hwy.
    R–Warfield
    L–Route M-55/watch traffic
    R–Route M-37
    R–10 Mile Rd.
    R–Merrillville
    L–Harvey Rd.

3   Irons/food services

4   Sand Lake Forest Campground/2½ miles north of Irons
    Continue west on Harvey Rd.
    L–Bass Lake Rd.

5   Bear Track River Campground
    R–Eight Mile Rd.
    Continue west on Freesoil Rd.
    R–Custer at Freesoil
    L–Hoague
    R–Quarterline
    R then L–continue north on Maple Rd.

6   Manistee/food services; fishing docks
    Return to Orchard Beach State Park

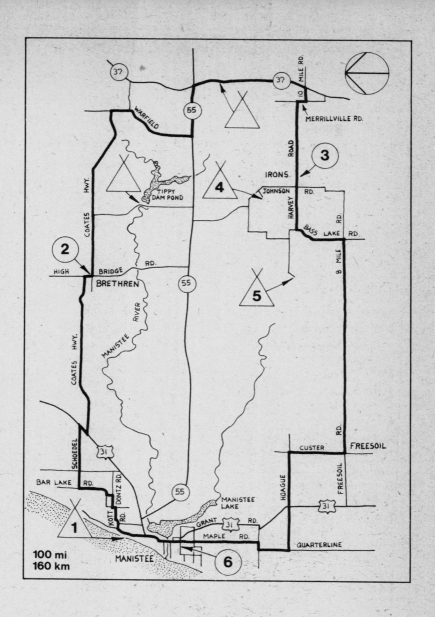

100 mi
160 km

143

Vermontville Maple Syrup Festival (#40)

EATON COUNTY, MICHIGAN

Length: *50 miles*

Terrain: *Level*

Points of Interest: *Michigan farm country, Maple Syrup Festival in early spring, apples in fall*

1 Start at the Farm Bureau parking lot beyond west end of Lansing on W. Saginaw St. Lansing/plane, bus, & train service; hostel (MSU Student Housing Co-ops, 311-B Student Services Bldg., East Lansing, MI 48823); food services; bike shop; state capitol
Go south on Canal Rd.
R–Vermontville Hwy.

2 Potterville/food services

3 Country Mill/R on Otto; apple cider and donuts in fall

4 Vermontville/food services; Maple Syrup Festival in early spring (parade, amusements, pancake breakfast, barbecued chicken)
Leave Vermontville east on Allegan
L–Brown Rd.
R–Bismark
L–Moore
L–Route 50 (Clinton Trail)
R–Mt. Hope Hwy.

5 Apple Schran/apple cider and donuts in fall
L–Oneida
R–St. Joe Hwy.
L–Canal Rd.
Return to Farm Bureau parking lot

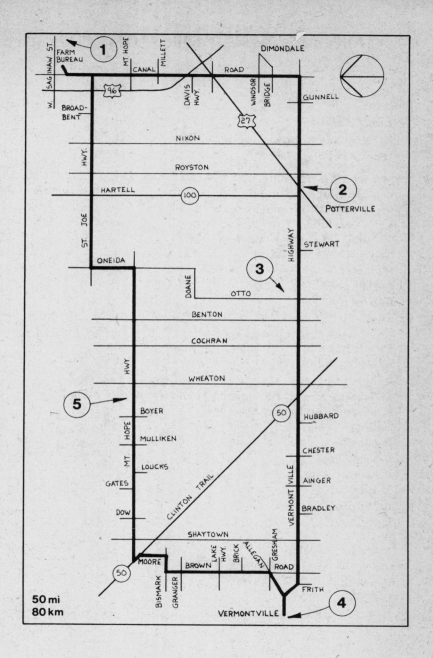

50 mi
80 km

145

Miller's Ice Cream Parlor Tour (#41)

INGHAM AND EATON COUNTIES, MICHIGAN

Length: *45 miles*
Terrain: *Level*
Points of Interest: *Michigan State University, Miller's Ice Cream Parlor in Eaton Rapids*

1 Start at MSU commuter Lot Y at intersection of Farm Lane and Mt. Hope Rd. in E. Lansing. East Lansing/bus service; hostel (MSU Student Housing Co-Ops, 311-B Student Services Bldg., E. Lansing, MI 48823); food services; bike shop; Michigan State Univ.
Go south on Farm Lane
R–Forest
L–College Rd.
R–Barnes Rd.
Continue onto East Barnes
R–Union
L–N. River
R–Knight/into Eaton Rapids
R–Mill

2 Miller's Ice Cream Parlor/open 11 am Sat. and 1 pm Sun.
Return on East Barnes & Barnes
L–Gale
R–Curtice
L–Onondaga
R–McCue
L–Eifert
R–Wilcox
L–Aurelius
R–Holt
Bear L onto Delhi
Continue onto Pine Tree
R–Sandhill
L–College Rd.
Return to Lot Y

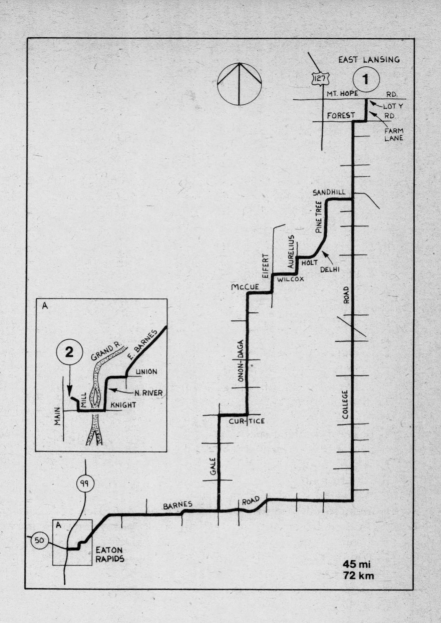

Tobico Marsh Tour (#42)

BAY COUNTY, MICHIGAN

Length: *33 miles*
Terrain: *Level*
Points of Interest: *Tobico Marsh, Bay City State Park, Museum of the Great Lakes, City Hall, Coast Guard lighthouse*

1 Start at Bay City City Hall at intersection of 10th & Washington/bus service; home hostel (1121 N. Birney, Bay City, MI 48706); food services; bike shop
Go north on Washington
L–7th Av.
Cross Bridge
R–Linn St. just after bridge
L–Midland St./west of town

2 Sage Library
R–Seven Mile Rd.
R–Beaver Rd.
L–Euclid

3 Bay City State Park/swimming
R–Killarney Beach Rd./along Tobico Marsh
Turn around at end of road
L–Euclid
L–Beaver Rd./along beach
R–State Park Dr./watch traffic
L–Wheeler Rd.
R–Patterson Rd.
L–Wilder Rd.
L–unimproved road at Dow Chemical out and back to Coast Guard lighthouse/just past RR tracks; ask permission to enter
L–Truman Pkwy./across Saginaw River
R–Center Av.

4 Museum of the Great Lakes
R–Madison
L–3rd St.
L–Water St.

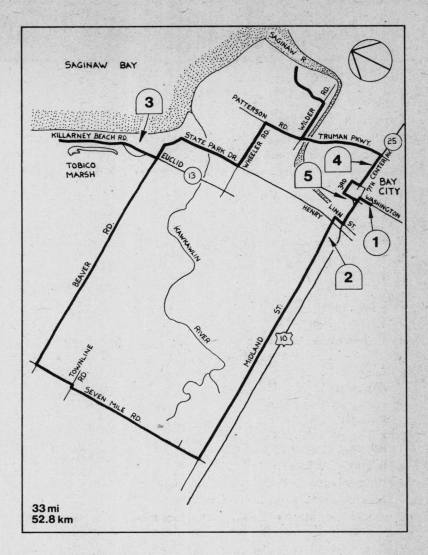

5 Wenonah Park
  L–7th Av.
  R–Washington
  Return to City Hall

Top of Ohio Bikeway (#43)

LOGAN COUNTY, OHIO

Length: *45 miles*

Terrain: *Rolling Hills*

Points of Interest: *highest point in Ohio, Zane Caverns, Ohio Caverns, old country towns.*

Special Note: *this bike route is signed for counterclockwise travel.*

1　Start at Marmon Valley Farm Hostel/Rt. 1, Zanesfield, OH 43360; northwest of Columbus off US 33
　Go west on County Route 153
　R–County Route 5 at Zanesfield
　R–County Route 2
　L–Route 292
　L–Route 540

2　Zane Caverns

3　Highest point in Ohio (el. 1,549 ft.)

4　Bellefontaine/bus service; food services; bike shop; Logan County Historical Museum
　Leave Bellefontaine east on County Route 10
　R–County Route T55
　L–County Route T182
　R–County Route 5
　L–County Route T1
　R–County Route 47
　R–into West Liberty

5　West Liberty/food services; farm center
　Leave West Liberty east on Route 245

6　Castel Platt Mac-O-Cheek/outstanding historical home open to the public for a fee

7　Ohio Caverns/largest natural caverns in Ohio
　L–Mt. Tabor Rd.
　R–County Route 28
　L–County Route 41
　Straight onto Route 287
　L–County Route 153 at Middleburg
　Cross US 33
　Return to Marmon Valley Farm Hostel

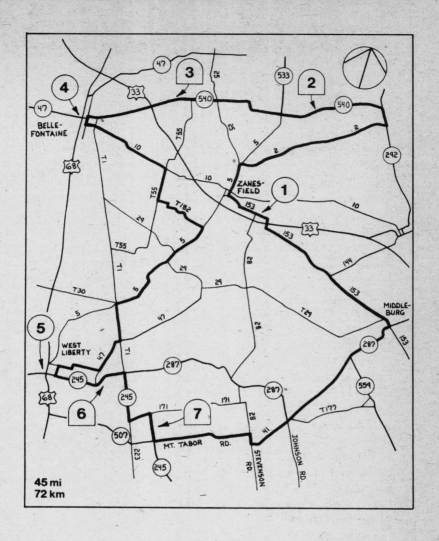

45 mi
72 km

151

Old Mill Bikeway (#44)

GREENE COUNTY, OHIO

Length: *35 miles*
Terrain: *Level*
Points of Interest: *Clifton Mill, John Bryan State Park, Grinnel Mill*
Special Note: *this bike route is signed for counterclockwise travel; do not confuse with signs for Little Miami Scenic River Bikeway.*

1   Start at Clifton Mill at southwest end of town/Clifton is south of
    Springfield on Route 72
    Follow bike route signs north along west end of town
    Continue north on T164
    Bear L—still T164
    Continue onto Hilt Rd. (30)
    L—Meredith Rd. (47)
    Continue south on Route 370

2   John Bryan State Park
    Bear R—Bryan Park Rd. (T18)
    Bear L—Grinnel Rd. (27)

3   Grinnel Mill
    R—Clifton Rd. (15)
    L—Clark Run Rd. (T31)
    L—Bradfute Rd. (10)
    L—Wilberforce-Clifton Rd. (94)
    R—Tarbox Cemetery Rd. (81)
    L—Conley Rd. (T35)
    R—Cedarville-Yellow Springs Rd. (12)
    L—through Cedarville
    Continue east on Barber Rd. (5)
    R—Townsley Rd. (83)
    L—Wildman Rd. (T177)
    R then L—Chillicothe Pike (T64)/cross US 42
    L—Battin Rd. (T61)
    Fork L—Cortsville Rd. (16)
    Bear R—Rife Rd. (67)
    L—South River Rd. (T152)
    Return to Clifton

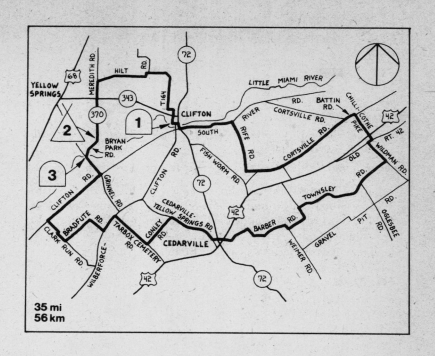

35 mi
56 km

153

Covered Bridge Bikeway (#45)

FAIRFIELD COUNTY, OHIO

Length: *37 miles*
Terrain: *Level*
Points of Interest: *covered wooden bridges, old locks of former Ohio & Erie Canal*
Special Note: *this bike route is signed for clockwise travel.*

1 Start at Rising Park near Route 37 on north end of Lancaster/ southeast of Columbus on US 33; food services
Go west to intersection of Fair Av. & Route 158/begin marked bike route
Continue west/becomes County Route 43
L—Wilson Rd. (45)
R—Mt. Zion Rd. (T183)
L—Lithopolis Rd. (39)

2 Covered Wooden Bridge/on Rock Mill Rd., 300 feet off bike route
R—Lithopolis-Winchester Rd. (6)
R—Waterloo Rd. (T197)

3 Covered Wooden Bridge over Little Walnut Creek
R—Hill Rd. (18)
Quick R, R again, then quick L—Waterloo-Eastern Rd. (T214)
R then L—Benadum Rd. (T210)
R—Pickerington Rd. (20)

4 Covered Wooden Bridge & Locks of former Ohio & Erie Canal
L—Lockville Rd. (T206)
Cross US 33
Continue east on Pleasantville Rd. (17)
L—Coakle Rd. (T255)/gravel
R—onto Bish Rd. (T255)

5 Covered Wooden Bridge on Bish Rd.
R—Havensport Rd. (T263)
L then R—Havensport Rd. (44)
Bear R—Election House Rd. (40)
L—Old Columbus Rd.
Bear R—onto Route 158
Return to Rising Park

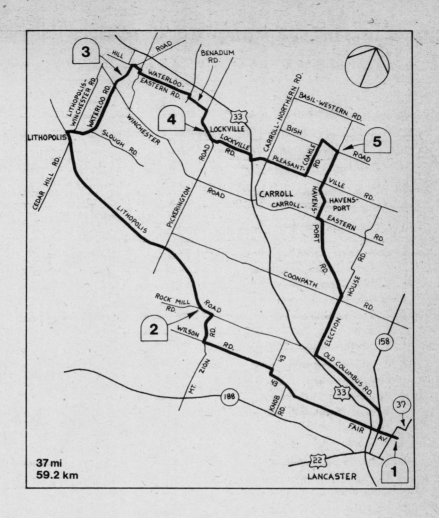

3

HILL ROAD

BENADUM RD.

WATERLOO-EASTERN RD.

LITHOPOLIS-WINCHESTER RD.

WATERLOO RD.

WINCHESTER

4

LOCKVILLE

33

LOCKVILLE RD.

CARROLL-NORTHERN RD.

BASIL-WESTERN RD.

BISH

COMLEY RD.

5

ROAD

PLEASANT-VILLE

LITHOPOLIS

CEDAR HILL RD.

SLOUGH RD.

ROAD

PICKERINGTON

ROAD

CARROLL

CARROLL-

HAVENS-PORT

HAVENS-PORT RD.

EASTERN

RD.

RD.

LITHOPOLIS

COONPATH

HOUSE RD.

ROCK MILL RD.

ROAD

2

WILSON RD.

RD.

MT. ZION

43

43

KNOB RD.

ELECTION

OLD COLUMBUS RD.

158

188

33

37

FAIR AV.

22

LANCASTER

1

37 mi
59.2 km

155

Tour of the Scioto River Valley (TOSRV) (#46)

FRANKLIN, PICKAWAY, ROSS, PIKE, AND SCIOTA COUNTIES, OHIO

Length: *105 miles one way*

Terrain: *Level to Rolling Hills*

Points of Interest: *Ohio Statehouse, Mound City Group National Monument*

Special Note: *the route below varies in some detail from the official TOSRV route; for information on how to participate in this annual two-day event, write Columbus Council-AYH, 125 Amazon Place, Columbus, OH 43209.*

1 Start at the Ohio Statehouse in Columbus at jct. of Broad & High Sts./plane & bus service; motels; food services; bike shops
Go south on High St.
R–Greenlawn
L–Harmon Av.
L–Frank Rd.
R (south)–Route 104

2 Chillicothe/motels; food services
Continue south on Route 104
Straight on Three Locks Rd. at jct. US 23
Bear R–Route 335
R–Clough at Waverly
L–US 23

3 Waverly/food services
Bear R–Route 104
Continue to Portsmouth

4 Portsmouth/motels; food services

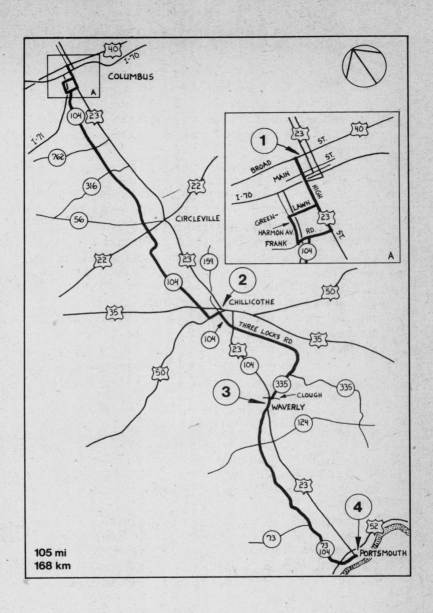

COLUMBUS

I-70

40

A

I-71

104 23

762

316

22

56

CIRCLEVILLE

22

23 159

104

35

104

23

104

50

335

335

CLOUGH

WAVERLY

124

23

73

4

52

73
104

PORTSMOUTH

1

23

40

BROAD ST.

ST.

MAIN

HIGH

I-70

LAWN

GREEN-
HARMON AV.
FRANK

RD.

ST.

104

23

A

2

CHILLICOTHE

THREE LOCKS RD.

35

50

3

4

105 mi
168 km

A LOOK AT TOSRV,
GRANDADDY OF AMERICA'S BICYCLE RALLIES

3,500 cyclists gather at the Ohio Statehouse every year in Columbus, Ohio, for what has become one of the world's bicycle touring classics. The two-day, 210-mile Tour of the Scioto River Valley, or "TOSRV" as it is better known, is sponsored by the Columbus Council of American Youth Hostels.

The Council provides a wide range of services to the riders. Trucks carry sleeping bags and other personal equipment to the overnight town of Portsmouth, Ohio; foodstops are located at twenty-five-mile intervals; a computerized registration system is used to process applications; indoor sleeping space is provided; a mobile radio/medical network is stretched along the route in case of injury

During TOSRV, weekend cyclists of every ability accumulate 700,000 rider miles, a distance equivalent to twenty-eight circumnavigations of the globe. Four hundred volunteer workers are the glue that holds it all together.

TOSRV was not always such a grand event. It started in 1962 when a father and son made the first ride down the valley. The idea caught on slowly, with a few more venturing out each year until 1966 when forty-five riders participated and AYH took over the sponsorship of the tour. Participation began to increase rapidly in 1967 when Charlie Pace, a Columbus banker and active AYH member, became director of the event. It was his organizational genius that built the tour into its current size.

As popular as TOSRV is, many cyclists prefer to ride the route without so much company. Even without the excitement of riding with an army of companion cyclists, the TOSRV route has something to offer the independent rider in the months after the big TOSRV weekend.

Transportation to the route is readily available into Columbus by bus or air. Overnight accommodations, restaurants, and groceries are plentiful along the route in

Circleville, Chillicothe, Waverly, and Portsmouth. Of course, an independent rider need not ride the route in a single day as some TOSRV riders do. Most of the route is flat, with a few hills between Chillicothe and Waverly, and can be ridden on a three-speed bicycle. Traffic is relatively light. Most through traffic is carried on Federal Route 23 which parallels the entire TOSRV route from Columbus to Portsmouth.

Several historic points are found along the way, including the Ohio Statehouse and the Mound City Group National Monument just north of Chillicothe. Chillicothe itself, the original capital of Ohio, contains many old, ornate buildings from the last century and offers a view of nearby Mt. Logan that was the inspiration for the Great Seal of Ohio. The most appealing aspect of the TOSRV route, however, is the simple beauty of the southern Ohio farm, pasture, and woodland. It is this beauty that draws 3,500 cyclists every year to the Scioto River Valley.

Southern Indiana Hoosier Hills (#47)

JEFFERSON AND RIPLEY COUNTIES, INDIANA

Length: *35 miles one way*
Terrain: *Rolling Hills to Hilly*
Points of Interest: *Versailles State Park, Clifty Falls State Park,* *Ohio River*
Special Note: *for a map of the entire Hoosier Hills Route write Dept. of Natural Resources, Division of Outdoor Recreation, 612 State Office Bldg., Indianapolis, IN 46204.*

1 Start at Clifty Falls State Park on Ohio River in southeastern Indiana/P.O. Box 847, Madison, IN 47250; swimming and hiking
   From Park Entrance turn R–Green Rd.
   L–Locust St.
   R–Pinehurst Av.
   L–Lanier Dr. (Route 7)
   R–Cross Av.
   L–Shun Pike Rd. (Route 100W)
   R–Route 400N/cross US 421
   L–Graham Rd. (Route 100E)
   Continue north on Route 250 to Canaan
   Continue north on Route 62
   L–Routes 62 & 129 to Cross Plains
   L–Route 900S at Cross Plains
   R–Benham Rd. (Route 50E)

2 Versailles/food services
   R–to Versailles State Park/cross Laughery Creek through Busching Covered Bridge

3 Versailles State Park/Versailles, IN 47042; boating, hiking, swimming, & fishing

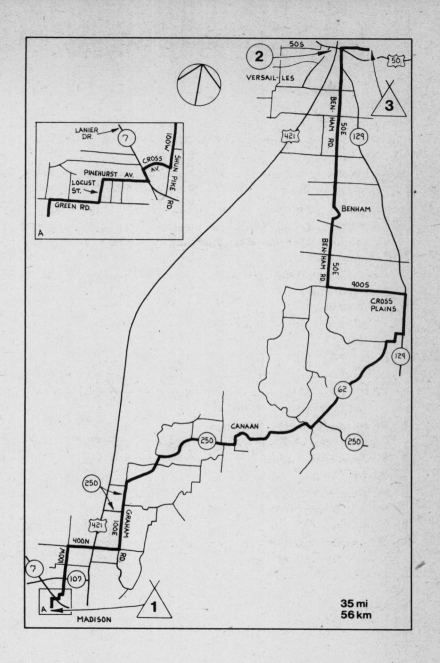

35 mi
56 km

Parke County Covered Bridges (#48)

PARKE COUNTY, INDIANA

Length: *32 miles*
Terrain: *Rolling Hills*
Points of Interest: *six covered bridges, Mansfield Roller Mill, Weise Mill, Spring Maple Fair, and Fall Covered Bridge Festival*
Special Note: *for more information write Parke County Tourist Information Center, Box 165, Rockville, IN 47872.*

1   Start at Rockville at jct. of US 36 & 41 in west-central Indiana/ bus service; motels; food services
    Go south on Route 29/under railroad trestle
    L–Route 144

2   Crooks Bridge/built in 1856 and rebuilt at present site in 1867
    Bear R–Route 121
    R–Route 30

3   McAllister's Bridge/built in 1914
    L–Route 29

4   Neet Bridge/built in 1904
    L–to Bridgeton

5   Weise Mill/built in 1823; still produces stone-ground cornmeal and whole wheat flour

6   Bridgeton Bridge/built in 1868
    Continue east on Route 20/along Big Raccoon Creek

7   Conley's Ford Bridge/built in 1906-1907
    Bear L–Route 47
    R–Route 24 to Mansfield
    L then R–across State Route 59

8   Mansfield Roller Mill/biult in 1820; recently restored

9   Mansfield Bridge/built in 1867
    Bear L (north)–Route 143
    Bear L–Route 32
    R–State Route 59
    L–Route 34
    Bear R–Route 121
    R–Route 29
    Return to Rockville

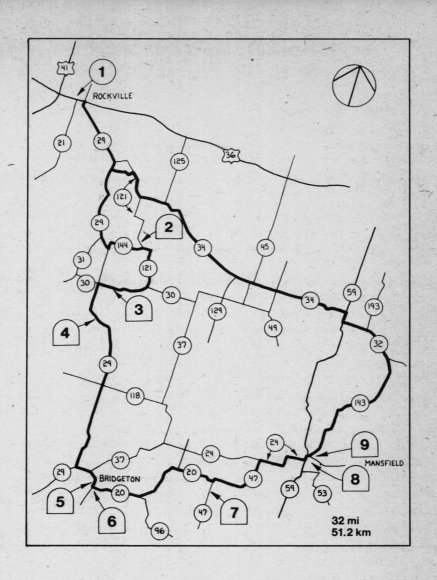

ROCKVILLE

41 1

21 29

125 36

121

29 2

144 34 45

31 121

30 30 34 59

129 193

3 32

4 49

29 37

118 143

24 9

37 24 MANSFIELD

29 BRIDGETON 20 47 8

5 20 59 53

6 47 7

96

32 mi
51.2 km

163

Chicago Lake Front Path (#49)

CHICAGO, ILLINOIS

Length: *20 miles one way*

Terrain: *Level*

Points of Interest: *Chicago skyline, Lake Michigan, waterfront parks*

Special Note: *Chicago is accessible by bus, train, and plane.*

Start at Bryn Mawr Av. (5600 North) just east of Lake Shore Dr.
Go south on Lake Front Path

1　Lincoln Park/Montrose Harbor, the Totem Pole, & Belmont Harbor are featured; Lincoln Park Zoo is south of Fullerton Av.

Continue south past Chicago Av. toward the Loop

Use east side path over bridge at Ohio St.

Continue south past Chicago River Locks

2　Grant Park/Buckingham Fountain, Shedd Aquarium, the Field Museum of Natural History, & the Adler Planatarium are featured

3　McCormick Place/Chicago's convention center

4　Museum of Science & Industry

5　Jackson Park

The Lake Front Path ends at South Shore Drive

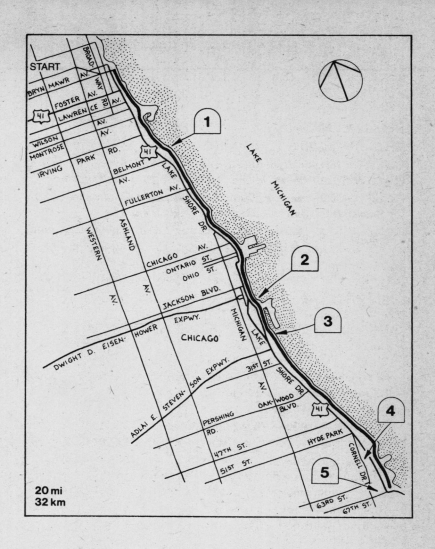

START

BRYN MAWR AV.

BROAD WAY

FOSTER AV. RD.

LAWRENCE AV.

41

AV.

WILSON AV.

MONTROSE

IRVING PARK RD.

41

WESTERN

ASHLAND

BELMONT AV.

FULLERTON AV.

LAKE

SHORE DR.

LAKE MICHIGAN

1

CHICAGO AV.

ONTARIO ST.

OHIO ST.

JACKSON BLVD.

AV.

AV.

EISEN- HOWER EXPWY.

DWIGHT D. EISEN-

CHICAGO

MICHIGAN

LAKE

2

3

ADLAI E. STEVEN- SON EXPWY.

31ST ST.

AV.

SHORE DR.

OAK- WOOD BLVD.

41

PERSHING RD.

47TH ST.

51ST ST.

HYDE PARK

CORNELL DR.

4

5

63RD ST.

67TH ST.

20 mi
32 km

Rock Island–Mississippi River Tour (#50)

ROCK ISLAND, MERCER, HENDERSON, AND HANCOCK COUNTIES, ILLINOIS

Length: *120 miles one way*

Terrain: *Rolling Hills*

Points of Interest: *Mississippi River, Black Hawk State Park, Big River State Forest, Delabar State Park, Nauvoo Historic Site*

Special Notes: *availability of food on this tour was not checked, so pack extra supplies; some gravel roads are used.*

1 Start at the County Courthouse and Centennial Bridge near 17th St. in Rock Island/train and bus service; motels; food services

Go south on 17th St. through Blackhawk State Park

2 Blackhawk State Park/museum
West on Route 92 (92nd Av.)
L (south) on Ridgewood Rd. to Taylor Ridge
Continue south on Route 94
Bear west on Route 94 at Reynolds
Continue west past southbound turn to Aledo/unpaved
L (south)–blacktop road to Joy
R (west)–Route 17
L (south)–to Keithsburg & Oquawka

3 Big River State Forest/boat rentals & fishing

4 Delabar State Park
Continue south on Route 164 to Gladstone
R–on Henderson access road toward river

5 Henderson County Conservation Area
Continue south to US 34
R–US 34/watch traffic
L (south)–Carman Blacktop Road to Lomax
R (west)–Route 96 to Dalles City & Nauvoo

6 Nauvoo/site of annual Labor Day Grape Festival; restored homes of Mormon leaders Joseph Smith and Brigham Young

7 Nauvoo Historic Site/boating, fishing, & museum

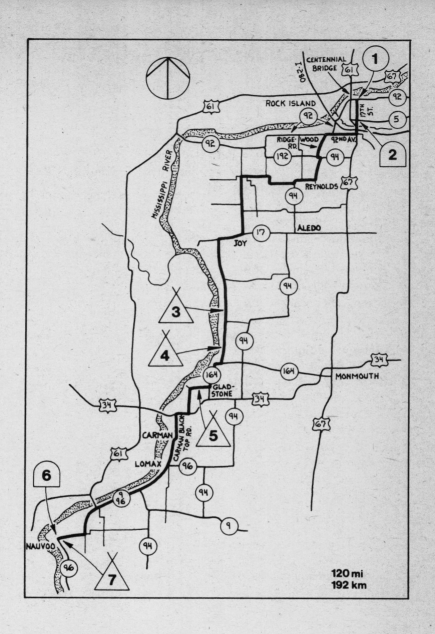

120 mi
192 km

Illinois River Route (#51)

GREENE, JERSEY, AND CALHOUN COUNTIES, ILLINOIS

Length: *63 miles*
Terrain: *Rolling Hills*
Points of Interest: *Pere Marquette State Park, Illinois River ferries, Mark Twain Wildlife Refuge, archeological museum and dig*

1 Start at Pere Marquette State Park on Route 100 near Grafton/ food services; horseback riding and boat rentals
Go east on Route 100 (Great River Rd.)
Cross Illinois River on Brussels Ferry
Go west on blacktop road to Brussels
R–at crossroads west of Brussels at church & cemetery
Continue north to Hardin & Kampsville

2 Kampsville/archeological museum displaying early Indian artifacts
Cross Illinois River on ferry
Continue on Route 108 to Eldred
R (south)–Eldred Rd.

3 Koster Site/archeological dig unearthing prehistoric settlements nearly 8,000 years old
Continue south on Route 100
Return to Pere Marquette State Park

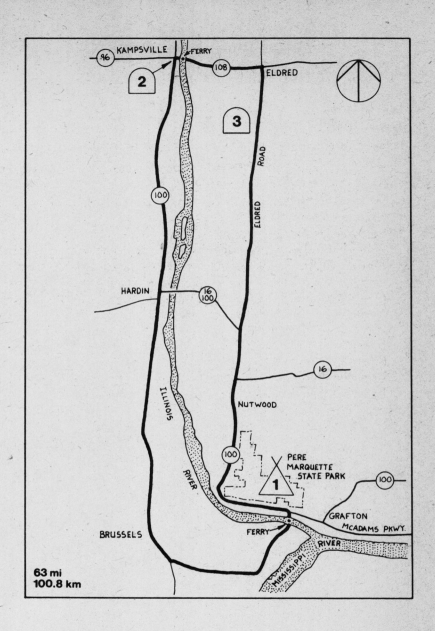

KAMPSVILLE   FERRY
96   **2**   108   ELDRED

3

100

E
L
D
R
E
D

R
O
A
D

HARDIN   16
100

16

NUTWOOD

100   PERE
MARQUETTE
STATE PARK

1

100

I
L
L
I
N
O
I
S

GRAFTON
MCADAMS PKWY.

R
I
V
E
R

BRUSSELS   FERRY

MISSISSIPPI   RIVER

63 mi
100.8 km

Levee–Bluffs Trail (#52)

MONROE COUNTY, ILLINOIS

Length: *80 miles*
Terrain: *Level*
Points of Interest: *Mississippi River, Fort De Chartres Historic Site*

Start at Columbia Airport near Columbia, Illinois, off Routes 3 &
    158 southeast of St. Louis, Missouri
Go south on Bluff Rd.

1 Valmeyer/food services

2 Fults/food services
   R–to Kidd and Fort De Chartres

3 Fort De Chartres Historic Site/French military installation that
    once controlled the Mississippi River Valley; museum
Continue west to Levee Rd.
North on Levee Rd./watch for gravel in places
Continue onto Route 156
L (north)–to Merrimac
R (east)–Bottom Rd.
L (north)–Bluff Rd.
Return to start

170

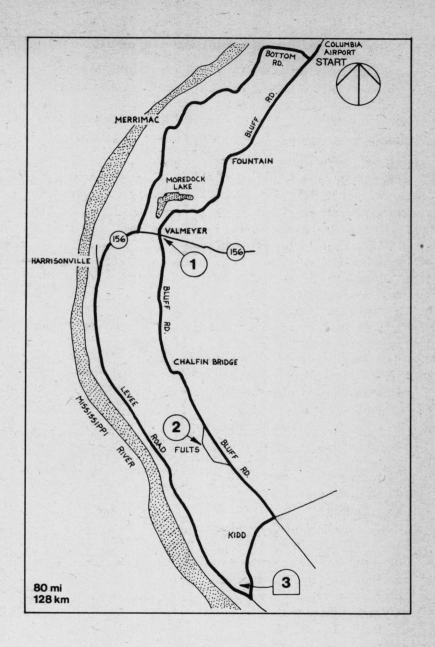

80 mi
128 km

Southern Illinois Great Rivers Tour (#53)

JACKSON, WILLIAMSON, JOHNSON, POPE, MASSAC, PULASKI, ALEXANDER, AND UNION COUNTIES, ILLINOIS

Length: *192 miles*

Terrain: *Rolling Hills to Hilly*

Points of Interest: *University of Southern Illinois, Shawnee National Forest, Ohio and Mississippi Rivers*

1. Start at Univ. of Southern Illinois at Carbondale/train and bus service; motels; food services; bike shops
Go east on Old Route 13
R (south)–Route 148
R (south)–Route 37

2. Goreville/food services

3. Ferne Clyffe State Park
South and east on Tunnel Hill Rd. at Goreville/go through railroad underpass
L–continue to Simpson & Glendale
R–Route 145/several steep hills before Lake Glendale

4. Dixon Springs State Park

5. Fort Massac State Park
R (west)–US 45/watch traffic

6. Metropolis/food services
L–Route 169
L–Route 37/follow Ohio River to Cairo

7. Cairo/food services

8. Fort Defiance State Park/former Civil War outpost used to blockade the Confederacy
North on Route 3

9. Horseshoe Lake Conservation Area

10. Union County Conservation Area
R–Route 146 at Ware

11. Anna/food services
L–US 51

12. Giant City State Park/cabins; fishing
Return to Carbondale

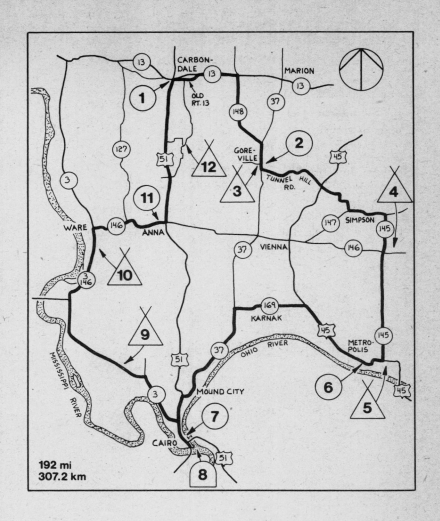

192 mi
307.2 km

173

Harrodsburg Loop (#54)

BOYLE AND MERCER COUNTIES, KENTUCKY

Length: *30 miles*
Terrain: *Rolling Hills*
Points of Interest: *Fort Harrod, Perryville Battlefield State Park, Kentucky countryside*

1 Start in Harrodsburg at jct. US 68 & 127 southwest of Lexington/bus service; motels; food services

2 Fort Harrod State Park
  Go west on Route 152
  L–Old Dixville Rd.
  R–US 68 to Perryville

3 Perryville/food services

4 Perryville Battlefield State Park/northwest of town on Route 1920
  East on Webster Rd.
  L–Route 34 to Danville

5 Danville/food services; Centre College
  L–Route 52
  R–Grass Rd. (Route 1915)
  R–US 68
  Return to Harrodsburg

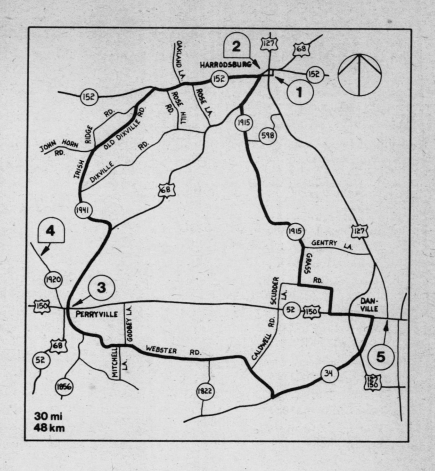

30 mi
48 km

175

Kentucky Bluegrass (#55)

CLARKE, MADISON, ESTILL, POWELL, AND WOLFE COUNTIES, KENTUCKY

Length: *176.5 miles*

Terrain: *Rolling Hills to Hilly*

Points of Interest: *Berea College, Fort Boonesborough State Park, Daniel Boone National Forest, Natural Bridge, Red River Gorge*

Special Note: *you will need a good front light to get through Nada Tunnel.*

1   Start at Berea, south of Lexington on US 25/bus service; motels; food services

2   Walnut Meadows Campground/Rt. 2, Berea, KY 40403

3   Berea College/founded in 1855, the college teaches folk arts and crafts of Appalachia
Go north on US 25
Bear R–Route 1016
L–US 421 to Richmond

4   Richmond/food services
North on Route 388

5   Fort Boonesborough State Park/Rt. 2, Richmond, KY 40475
R (north)–Route 627

6   Winchester/food services
R (east)–Route 15

7   Stanton/food services
Continue south on Route 11

8   Natural Bridge State Resort Park/Slade, KY 40376
Continue south on Route 11
L–Route 715/continue north through Pine Ridge

9   Red River Gorge
Bear L–Route 77

10   Nada Tunnel/an old railroad tunnel; use a good front light
R (north)–Route 11
L–Route 82 at Clay City
Bear L–Route 89 at Hargett

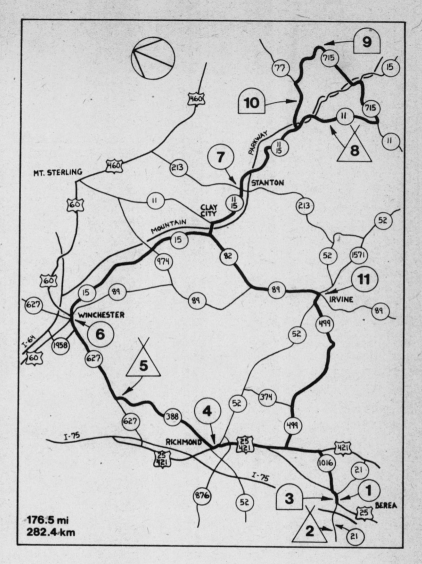

11 Irvine/food services
R–Route 52
L–Route 499/rough road in places
L–US 421
R–Route 1016
Return to Berea

Minnesota

56

57

58

59

Manitoba–Minnesota Tour (#56)

MANITOBA PROVINCE, CANADA
KITTSON COUNTY, MINNESOTA

Length: *123 miles one way*

Terrain: *Level*

Points of Interest: *Winnipeg, St. Pierre, St. Malo Park and Pioneer Museum, Tolstoi, US-Canadian Border, Lake Bronson State Park*

1 Start at City Hall in Winnipeg on Main St. just north of downtown/plane, train, & bus service; motels; food services
Go south on Main St. (Route 52)
Bear L–St. Anne's Rd. (Route 150)
L–Route 165
R (south)–Route 59 (Lagimodiere Blvd.)

2 St. Pierre/hosts Frog Follies in early August where the Canadian Frog Jumping Championship is the main event; food services

3 St. Malo/bus service; food services; pioneer museum

4 St. Malo Park

5 US-Canadian Border & Customs/bring proper identification
Continue south on US 59

6 Lake Bronson/food services

7 Lake Bronson State Park

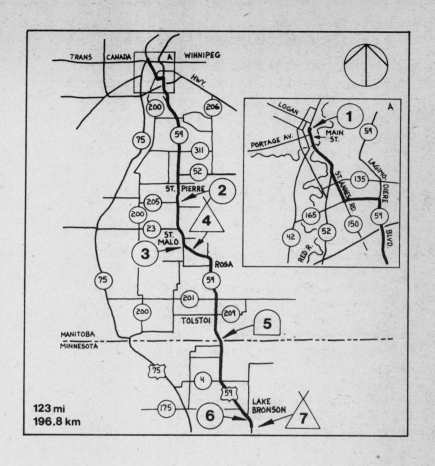

123 mi
196.8 km

St. Croix River Tour (#57)

CHICAGO AND PINE COUNTIES, MINNESOTA
POLK AND BURNETT COUNTIES, WISCONSIN

Length: *93 miles*

Terrain: *Rolling Hills*

Points of Interest: *Interstate Park, St. Croix State Park, St. Croix River*

1. Start at Interstate Park, south of St. Croix Falls, Wisconsin, off US 8 northeast of Minneapolis-St. Paul

2. St. Croix Falls/food services
   Go north on Route 87
   Continue north on Route 48 to Grantsburg

3. Grantsburg/food services
   Continue north on County Route F at Grantsburg
   L (west)–Route 77
   Cross St. Croix River into Minnesota
   Continue west on Route 48
   South on County Route 22 to St. Croix State Park

4. St. Croix State Park
   Continue west on Route 48
   L–Route 23 at Hinkley/go three miles
   L–County Route 61 to Pine City

5. Pine City/food services
   Continue south on Route 361
   Continue south on County Route 30
   L–County Route 9 at Harris
   Bear L (east)–County Route 20
   L–County Route 82
   Continue east on US 8 through Taylors Falls
   Cross St. Croix River
   Return to Interstate Park

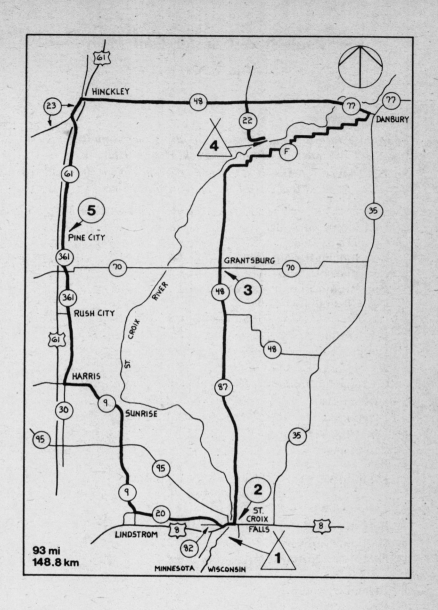

93 mi
148.8 km

St. Paul–State Capitol Tour (#58)

ST. PAUL, MINNESOTA

Length: *17 miles*

Terrain: *Level*

Points of Interest: *Minnesota State Capitol, Mississippi River, Fort Snelling State Park, Highland Park, Harriet Island Park*

Special Note: *this tour is best taken on weekends when city traffic is light; St. Paul is accessible by plane, train, & bus.*

1 Start at the State Capitol on University Av. (US 12) off I-35E in downtown St. Paul

Go south on Park St.

Bear R–John Ireland Blvd.

Continue onto Summit Av.

Bear R–onto Summit Pkwy.

L–Mississippi River Blvd.

Use sidewalk on W. 7th St. Bridge to Fort Snelling

2 Fort Snelling State Park

L–onto Edgecumbe Rd.

R–continue on Edgecumbe Rd.

Continue north through Highland Park

3 Highland Park

R–Jefferson

L–Lexington Pkwy.

R–St. Clair Av.

Bear L–W. 7th St.

R–Smith Av. (Route 49)/cross Mississippi River

L–Ohio St. opposite Cherokee Av.

L–Plato Blvd.

R–Nagasaki Rd.

4 Harriet Island Park

L–Wabasha St./cross Mississippi River

L–12th St.

R–John Ireland Blvd.

Return to State Capitol

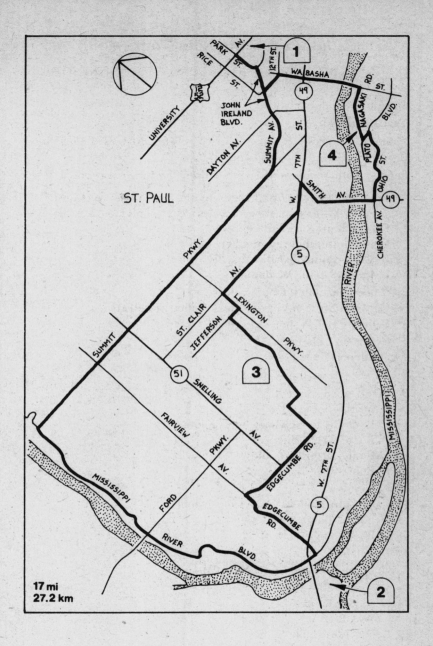

Southeast Minnesota Tour (#59)

HOUSTON AND FILMORE COUNTIES, MINNESOTA

Length: *106 miles one way*
Terrain: *Rolling Hills*
Points of Interest: *Mississippi River, Beaver Creek Valley State Park, Forestville State Park*
Special Note: *some county roads on this tour are not signed.*

1   Start at La Crescent off I-90 opposite La Crosse, Wisconsin, on the Mississippi River/bus service; motel; food services
Go south from La Crescent
Continue south on Route 26 to Brownsville
R (west)–Route 3 at Brownsville
R–Route 249 to Caledonia

2   Caledonia/motel; food services
Continue west to Beaver Creek Valley State Park

3   Beaver Creek Valley State Park
Return to Caledonia
South on Route 44

4   Spring Grove/motel; food services

5   Mabel/food services
R (north)–Route 43
L–Route 24 to Newburg and Lenora
R–Route 23 at Lenora
L–Route 12 for two miles
R–Route 21 to Lanesboro
R–US 16

6   Lanesboro/food services; trout hatchery
L (north)–Route 250
L–Route 8 to Fountain

7   Fountain/food services
Continue west on Route 80 to Wykoff

8   Wykoff/food services
L (south)–Route 5
Cross US 16
L–into Forestville State Park

9   Forestville State Park

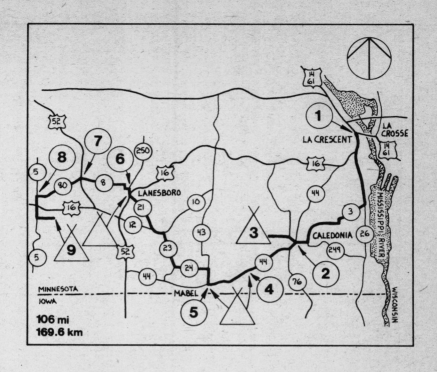

CHAPTER NINE
Southern Plains

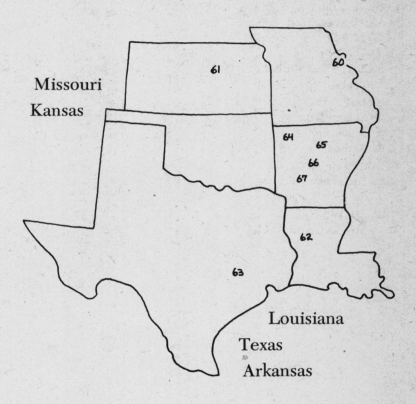

Missouri
Kansas

Louisiana
Texas
Arkansas

St. Louis Downtown Parks Tour (#60)

ST. LOUIS, MISSOURI

Length: *14 miles*

Terrain: *Level*

Points of Interest: *Gateway Arch, Forest Park, Tower Grove Park, Lyon Park*

Special Note: *ride this tour on Sunday when traffic is light.*

1   Start at the Gateway Arch off I-70 on the Mississippi River
Go west on Market St.
R–12th St.
L–Olive St.
Bear L–Lindell Blvd.
L–Kingshighway Blvd.

2   Forest Park
R–Shaw Blvd.
L–Mackland
L–Arsenal St.

3   Tower Grove Park
L–Broadway

4   Lyon Park
R–Market St.
Return to Gateway Arch

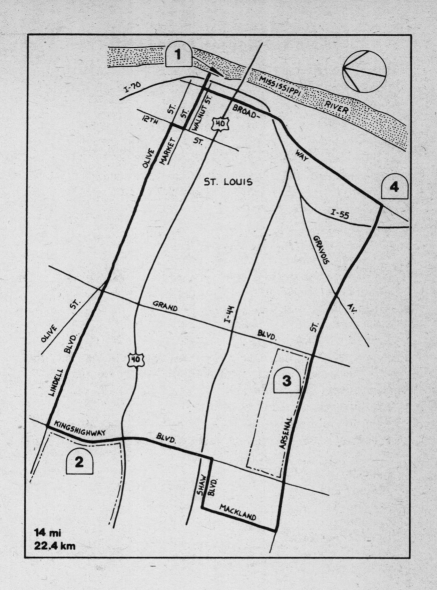

14 mi
22.4 km

191

Central Kansas Tour (#61)

SALINE, ELLSWORTH, LINCOLN, RUSSELL, MITCHELL, OSBORNE, CLOUD, CLAY, AND DICKINSON COUNTIES, KANSAS

Length: *315 miles*

Terrain: *Level to Rolling Hills*

Points of Interest: *The Eisenhower Center in Abilene, Old Abilene Town, Kanopolis–Mushroom Rock State Park, Wilson State Park, Glen Elder State Park*

1 Start in Abilene, 153 miles west of Kansas City on I-70/bus service; motels; food services; The Eisenhower Center; Old Abilene Town
Go west on Route 221 through Solomon & New Cambria
Continue on Pacific Street into Salina

2 Salina/bus service; motels; food services; bike shop
West on Route 140
L (south)–Route 141

3 Kanopolis–Mushroom Rock State Park/swimming, fishing; the Mushroom Rock area is 8 miles north of the campground
Continue west on Route 140

4 Ellsworth/food services; Rogers House museum
Continue west on road to Wilson

5 Wilson/opera house; annual After Harvest Czech Festival held on last Saturday in July
R (north)–Route 232

6 Wilson State Park
R–Route 18
L–Route 181
R–US 24 at Downs

7 Glen Elder State Park
Bear L–Route 9

8 Concordia/food services
Continue east on Route 9
R–Route 15

9 Clay Center/food services; Arts & Craft show in late September
R–Route 197 to Industry

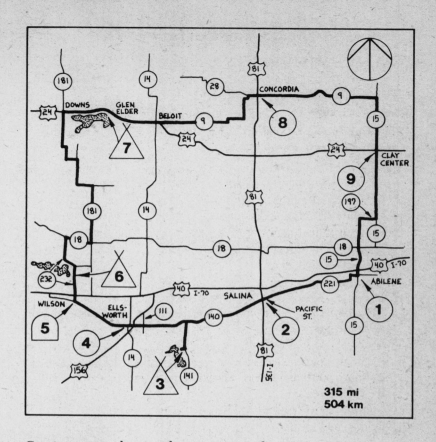

Continue west, then south on county road
Continue south on Route 15
Return to Abilene

Chain Gang Century (#62)

NATCHITOCHES PARISH, LOUISIANA

Length: *103 miles*
Terrain: *Hilly*
Points of Interest: *Northwestern State University, Kisatchie National Forest*

1 Start at Northwestern State University campus in Natchitoches/
  bus service; motels; food services
  Go west on Route 6
  L–Route 117 at Hagewood
  L–Route 120 at Provencal

2 Provencal/food services
  R–Route 478 at Flora

3 Flora/food services
  L–Route 117
  R–Route 418/opposite Forest Service office; cross cattle guard
  R–Route 117
  L–Route 118 at Kisatchie

4 Kisatchie/food services
  L–Route 506/paved road; unsigned; go ½ mile
  R–still Route 506
  Continue north on Route 119 at Gorum

5 Derry/food services
  Continue on Route 119
  Bear L––Route 484
  L–Route 494
  Cross Route 1 to Cypress
  R (west)–Route 120
  R–Route 478 at Flora
  L–Route 230, just after Old River bridge/unsigned
  L–Route 1 Bypass
  R–Route 6
  Return to Northwestern State University

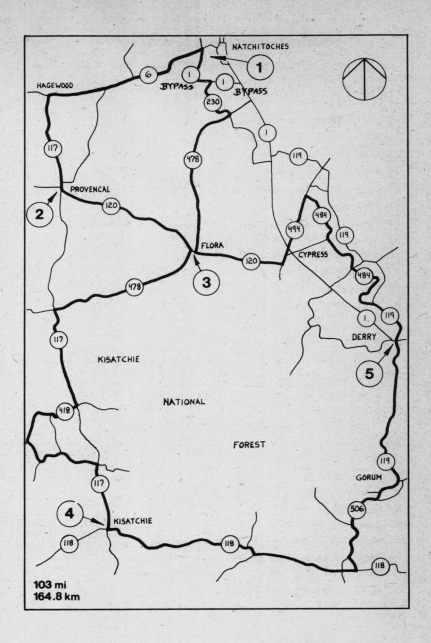

Southeastern Texas Tour (#63)

HARRIS, AUSTIN, FAYETTE, BASTROP, AND TRAVIS COUNTIES, TEXAS

Length: *180 miles one way*

Terrain: *Rolling Hills to Hilly*

Points of Interest: *Texas State Capitol at Austin, Bastrop and Buescher State Parks*

Special Note: *water on parts of this tour is scarce, so pack an extra supply.*

Start at jct. of US 290 & Route 529 northwest of Houston
Go west on Route 529/no trees or water for 20 miles
R–Route 362 North
L–Route 529 West

1 Sunnyside/food services; water
2 Burleigh/food services; water
3 Bellville/food services; water
4 Camping in Bellville City Park at top of hill
West on Route 159 toward Nelsonville/small towns with food & water about every 10 miles
5 Fayetteville/food services; water
Continue north on Route 159 toward Oldenburg
L–Route 159 to La Grange
6 La Grange/food services; water
North on US 77
L–Route 153 toward Winchester/steep hills
7 Smithville/food services
R–Route P1/winding, hilly road
8 Buescher State Park
9 Bastrop State Park
R–Route 71/heavy traffic; side shoulder
10 Bastrop/food services; water
R–Route 969/30 miles to Austin
Route 969 becomes Martin Luther King Jr. Blvd.
11 Enter Austin/plane, bus, and train service; motels; food services; bike shops; Texas State Capitol; University of Texas

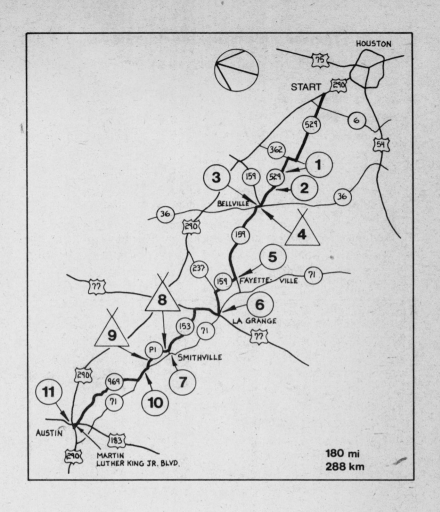

180 mi
288 km

Devil's Den State Park (#64)

WASHINGTON COUNTY, ARKANSAS

Length: *26 miles one way*

Terrain: *Hilly*

Points of Interest: *Devil's Den State Park, swimming, fishing, hiking, caving*

1   Start at jct. of US 71 & Route 265 South in Fayetteville/plane & bus service; motels; food services
Go south on Route 265 through Hogeye & Strickler
R–Route 170

2   Mountain Top Grocery/only food service on route

3   Devil's Den State Park/cabins, lodge, & restaurant available; swimming, fishing, hiking, & caving

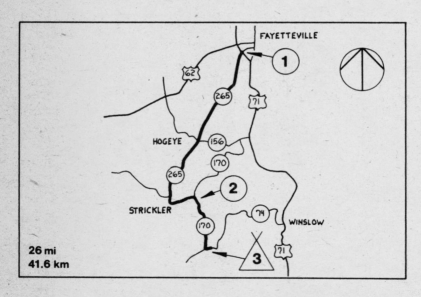

Blanchard Springs Caverns Tour (#65)

STONE AND BAXTER COUNTIES, ARKANSAS

Length: *54 miles*

Terrain: *Rolling Hills to Hilly*

Points of Interest: *Ozark Folk Culture Center in Mountain View, Blanchard Springs Caverns, Ozark National Forest*

1 Start at Mountain View at jct. of Routes 5 & 9 in north-central Arkansas/motels; food services

2 Ozark Folk Culture Center/arts & crafts displays, shows every night except Sunday during late spring, summer, & fall; Arkansas Folk Festival on second, third, & fourth weekend of April; write Ozark Folk Center, Mountain View, AR 72560

   Go north on Route 9

   L–Route 14 at Allison/uphill

3 Blanchard Springs Caverns

4 Big Flat/food services

   L–Route 263

   L–Route 66 at Timbo

   Return to Mountain View

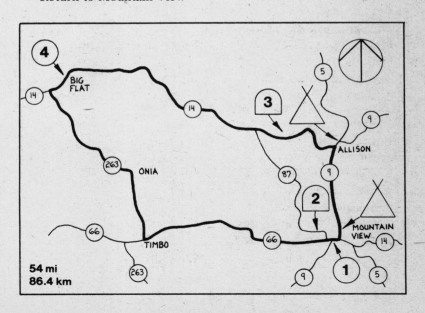

Arkansas–Ozarks Tour (#66)

PULASKI, FAULKNER, WHITE, CLEBURNE, STONE, IZARD, BAXTER, MARION, BOONE, NEWTON, POPE, YELL, PERRY, GARLAND, AND SALINE COUNTIES, ARKANSAS

Length: *457 miles*

Terrain: *Rolling Hills to Hilly*

Points of Interest: *Arkansas State Capitol in Little Rock, Ozark Folk Culture Center in Mountain View, Bull Shoals State Park, Buffalo River, Dardanelle State Park, Hot Springs National Park*

Special Note: *this is a rugged 7-to-9-day tour with daily distances of 54 to 74 miles.*

1 Start at the State Capitol building in Little Rock/plane, train, & bus service; motels; food services; bike shops
Go north on Woodlane St.
R–4th St.
L–Broadway
Cross Broadway Bridge to North Little Rock
R–continue on Broadway
L–Main St.
Continue north on Route 107

2 Burns Park/west of North Little Rock on Arkansas River
L–US 64
R–Route 36/continue through Mt. Vernon
L (north)–Route 124
Bear R (north)–Route 107
R–Route 25
L–Route 16
Cross Narrows bridge at Greers Ferry Lake

3 Greers Ferry/motels; food services
Stay on Route 16/begin long uphill to Shirley

4 Shirley/food services
R–Route 9/uphill to Rushing

5 Mountain View/motels; food services

6 Ozark Folk Culture Center/arts & crafts displays, shows every

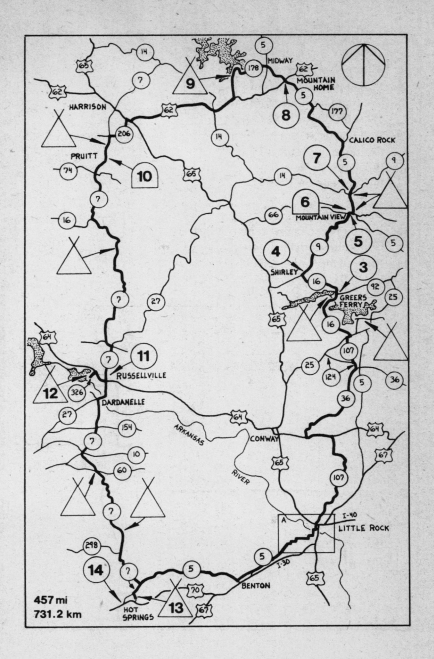

457 mi
731.2 km

night except Sunday during late spring, summer, & fall
Continue north on Route 5 to Mountain Home

7 Allison/food services

8 Mountain Home/motels; food services
Continue on Route 5 to Midway
West on Route 178 at Midway

9 Bull Shoals State Park/14 miles from Mountain Home
Continue on Route 178
R–US 62
R–Continue on US 62 & 65
L–Route 206
L–Route 7

10 Buffalo River/canoe rentals at Pruitt
Continue south on Route 7 to Russellville

11 Russellville/motels; food services
R–US 64

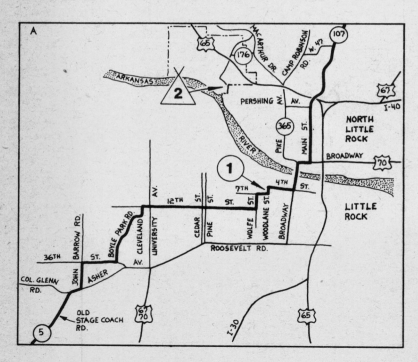

L–Route 326

12 Dardanelle State Park
Return to Russellville
R (south)–Route 7/hilly through Ouachita Mtns.
R–Route 7 at Fountain Lake
L–US 70B into Hot Springs National Park

13 Gulpha Gorge Camping Area

14 Hot Springs/motels; food services; bike shop; thermal baths
Return to Route 7
R (east)—Route 7
Continue on Route 5 to Benton
Go northeast along west side of I-30 on frontage road at
Benton
Continue on Route 5 into Little Rock
R–Col. Glenn Rd. & Asher Av. (Route 300)/heavy traffic
L–John Barrow Rd.
R–36th St.
L–Boyle Park Rd./through Boyle Park
L–Cleveland
R–12th St./go two miles
L–Wolfe St.
R–7th St.
L–Woodlane St.
Return to State Capitol

DeGray Lake Circuit (#67)

CLARK AND HOT SPRINGS COUNTIES, ARKANSAS

Length: *67 miles*
Terrain: *Rolling Hills*
Points of Interest: *DeGray Lake and Dam, DeGray State Park*

1 Start at DeGray State Park northwest of I-30 and Arkadelphia on
 Route 7
 Go L from park on Route 7
 L–Route 84 at Bismarck

2 Amity/food services
 L–Route 8 at Amity

3 Arkadelphia/motels; food services
 L–US 67 at Arkadelphia
 Bear L–Route 7 at Caddo Valley

4 DeGray Lake Dam
 Return to DeGray State Park

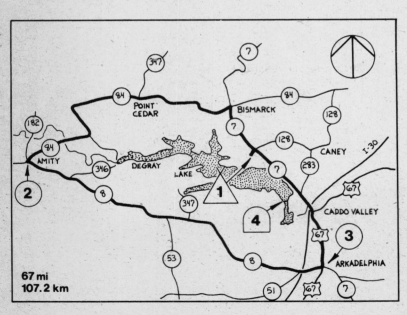

CHAPTER TEN

Northwest

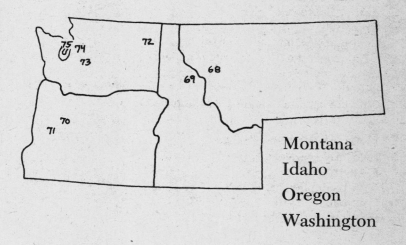

Montana
Idaho
Oregon
Washington

Missoula–Bitterroot Mountains Tour (#68)

MISSOULA COUNTY, MONTANA

Length: *78 miles*

Terrain: *Hilly*

Points of Interest: *University of Montana, Clark Fork, Lolo National Forest, Bitterroot Mountains*

1 Start at the Birchwood Hostel/600 S. Orange St., Missoula, MT 59801; plane & bus service; food services; bike shops; University of Montana

   Go north on Orange St.

   L (west)–Broadway St. (US 93)

   Bear L–Route 263

   Cross I-90

   Continue west on frontage road

   Continue west onto I-90/watch traffic

   R–onto frontage road

   L–Petty Creek Rd./unpaved

   Continue on Graves Creek Rd./unpaved

   L–US 12/watch for truck traffic

2 Lewis & Clark Campground

3 Lolo/food services

   L–US 93

   Bear L–Stephens St. (US 93)

   Continue onto Orange St. (US 93)

   Return to the Birchwood Hostel

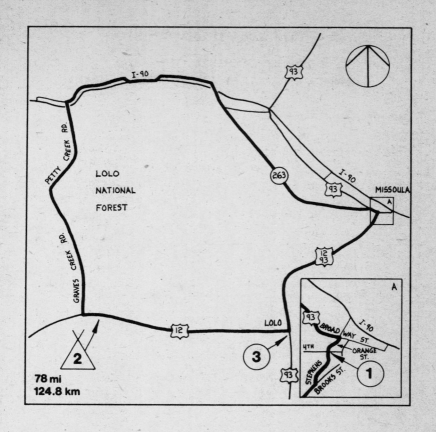

LOLO
NATIONAL
FOREST

I-90

93

263

I-90

93

MISSOULA

A

12
93

PETTY CREEK RD.

GRAVES CREEK RD.

12

LOLO

93

2

3

78 mi
124.8 km

93

BROADWAY ST.

I-90

4TH

ORANGE ST.

STEPHENS

BROOKS ST.

1

A

Explorers Route (#69)

MISSOULA COUNTY, MONTANA
CLEARWATER AND LEWIS COUNTIES, IDAHO

Length: *214 miles one way*
Terrain: *Hilly*
Points of Interest: *Lolo Hot Springs, Lolo Pass, Route of Lewis and Clark, Lochsa Wilderness Area, Nez Perce Indian Reservation*
Special Note: *few food services are available between Missoula, Montana, and Kooskia, Idaho; Forest Service campsites are located at 10-20 mile intervals between Lolo, Montana, and Lowell, Idaho.*

1 Start at the Birchwood Hostel/600 S. Orange St., Missoula, MT 59801; bus & plane service; motels; food services; bike shops; University of Montana
  Go south on Orange St.
  Continue on Stephens St.
  R—Brooks (US 93 & 12)
  Continue south on US 93 & 12

2 Lolo/food services
  R—US 12/long climb to Lolo Pass; watch for heavy truck traffic

3 Lolo Hot Springs/food services; last food for 85 miles

4 Lolo Pass (el. 5,233 ft.)

5 Lowell/motel; food services

6 Syringa/motel; food services

7 Kooskia/food services
  R—continue on US 12

8 Kamiah/motel; food services

9 Orofino/motel; food services

10 Myrtle Beach Campground/food services
   Continue west on US 12 & 95
   Bear L—continue on US 12 to Lewiston

11 Lewiston/plane & bus service; motels; food services; bike shop

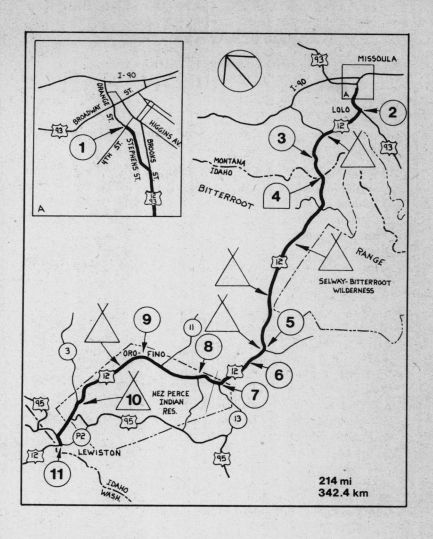

214 mi
342.4 km

Gingerbread Ride (#70)

MARION COUNTY, OREGON

Length: *41.5 miles one way*
Terrain: *Rolling Hills*
Points of Interest: *Oregon State Capitol, Gingerbread Cafe, North Santiam River*

1   Start at State Capitol building in Salem, south of Center St. at Summer St. N.E./bus service; motels; food services; bike shop
     Go east on Court St.
     Cross bike pedestrian bridge just past 20th St.
     R–21st St.
     L–State St./proceed on sidewalk past Oregon State Prison to bike path
     R–Lancaster Dr.
     L–Macleay Rd.
     R–Cordon Rd.
     L–Lancaster Dr.
     R–Deer Park/uphill; pass Western Baptist Bible College
     L–Turner Rd.
     Continue on Marion Rd.
     Continue on Shaff Rd. at 70th Av.
     R–N. Gardner Av. at Stayton
     L–Washington St.
     L–6th St.
     R–Jefferson
     L–10th Av.
     R–E. Santiam/cross Route 22
     Continue onto Old Mehama Rd.
     L–Route 22
     R–Ferry Rd.
     L–Grove at P.J.'s Market
     R–Gingerbread St.

2   Mehama Gingerbread House/excellent food
     R–Route 22
     L–Little North Fork Rd.

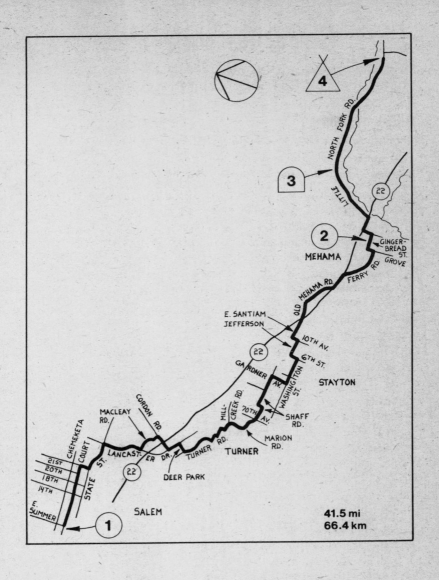

3 North Fork Park / L down steep gravel road; swimming
  Stay on Little North Fork Rd. / becomes hilly
4 Elkhorn Valley Recreation Site

Central Oregon Coast (#71)

DOUGLAS, LANE, LINN, BENTON, POLK, AND LINCOLN
COUNTIES, OREGON

Length: *280 miles*

Terrain: *Rolling Hills to Very Hilly*

Points of Interest: *University of Oregon, Willamette Valley, Oregon coast, Sea Lion Caves, Siuslaw National Forest*

1 Start at the University of Oregon in Eugene/plane, train, & bus service; motels; food services; bike shops
  Go north on Agate St. to Willamette River
  Continue on bike path across Willamette River
  L–continue on bike path along river
  Bear R–under I-105
  L–Oakway
  R–Cal Young Rd.
  L–Coburg Rd.

2 Armitage State Park
  R then L–across Willamette St. onto E. Van Duyne
  Continue north on River Rd.
  L–LaSalle St. at Harrisburg

3 Harrisburg/food services
  R–Third St.
  Continue north on Piena Rd.
  L–Route 34/cross Willamette River
  Continue on Harrison Blvd.

4 Corvallis/bus service; motels; food services; Oregon State Univ.
  R–Route 99W
  L–Route 22 at Rickreall/climb over Coast Range

5 Rickreall/food services; bike shop
  Bear L (west)–Route 18
  L–US 101/south along Oregon Coast

6 Devils Lake State Park

7 Lincoln City/food services; bike shop

8 Beverly Beach State Park

9 Newport/food services

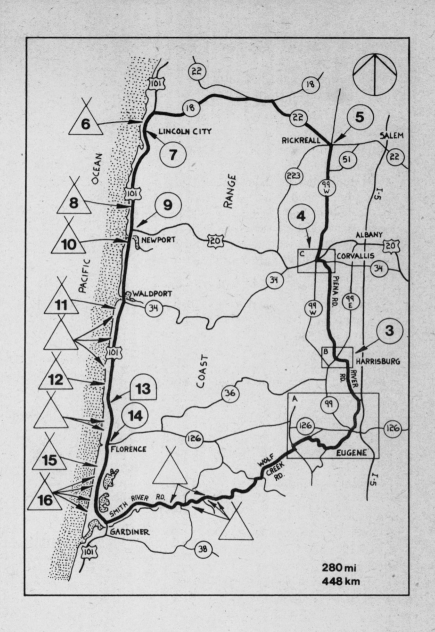

280 mi
448 km

10   South Beach State Park
11   Beachside State Park
12   Washburne Memorial State Park
13   Sea Lion Caves/private park
14   Florence/food services; bike shop
15   Honeyman Memorial State Park
16   Oregon Dunes National Recreation Area
    L–Smith River Rd. at Gardiner/no stores until Eugene; steep climb through Oxbow Burn to Oxbow Pass (el. 1,250 ft.)
    R–unsigned road
    L–unsigned (Wolfe Creek Rd.)/uphill
    L–unsigned (Territorial Hwy.)
    R–Crow Rd.
    R–Erickson Rd. at Petzoldt Rd./gravel
    R–Pine Grove Rd.
    L–Spencer Creek Rd.
    Continue onto Loman Hwy. at Bailey Hill Rd./becomes E. 29th Av.
    L–Amazon Pkwy.
    R–E. 24th Av.
    L–Agate St.
    Return to University of Oregon campus

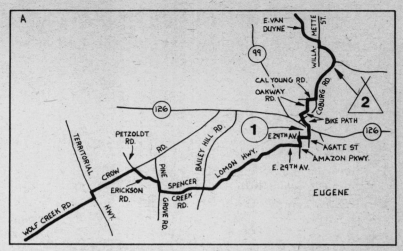

A

E. VAN DUYNE

99

WILLA-METTE ST.

CAL YOUNG RD.
OAKWAY RD.

COBURG RD.

2

126

1

BIKE PATH

126

E. 24TH AV.

AGATE ST
AMAZON PKWY.

E. 29TH AV.

PETZOLDT RD.

RD.

BAILEY HILL RD.

LOMON HWY.

TERRITORIAL

CROW

PINE

SPENCER

GROVE RD.

CREEK RD.

EUGENE

ERICKSON RD.

WOLF CREEK RD.

HWY.

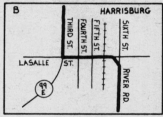

B

HARRISBURG

THIRD ST.
FOURTH ST.
FIFTH ST.
SIXTH ST.

LASALLE

ST.

RIVER RD.

99 E

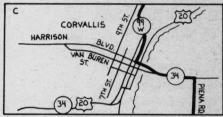

C

CORVALLIS

9TH ST.

99 W

20

HARRISON

BLVD.

VAN BUREN ST.

34

7TH ST.

PIENA RD.

34

20

Spokane–Roosevelt Lake Tour (#72)

SPOKANE, PEND OREILLE, STEVENS, AND LINCOLN COUNTIES, WASHINGTON

Length: *257 miles*

Terrain: *Rolling Hills to Hilly*

Points of Interest: *Spokane, Pend Oreille State Park, Fort Colville, Roosevelt Lake, Fort Spokane, and Spokane Plains Battlefield*

1 Start in downtown Spokane/plane, bus, & train service; motels; food services; bike shops

2 Riverside Park/3 miles northwest of town on Spokane River; 5,514 acres include "Indian Rock Paintings" and "Spokane House"
Go north on US 2 (Division St.)

3 Pend Oreille State Park

4 Newport/motels; food services
L (north)–Route 20 at Newport/follow Pend Oreille River

5 Usk/food services
L (west)–at Tiger/still Route 20

6 Colville/motels; food services

7 Kettle Falls/food services
L (south)–Route 25/steep grades and good views along Roosevelt Lake

8 Hunters/food services

9 Hunters Park/about 2 miles west of town; swimming

10 Fort Spokane/old frontier army post in 1880s and 90s; camping & food services nearby

11 Davenport/motels; food services
L (east)–US 2

12 Reardan/motels; food services
US 2 is very steep at Deep Creek
US 2 divides into 4-lane highway at Fairchild AFB/watch traffic

13 Spokane Plains Battlefield/10 miles west of Spokane
Continue onto Sunset Blvd. (Bus. US 2)/moderately steep grade
Continue east on Third St. into downtown Spokane

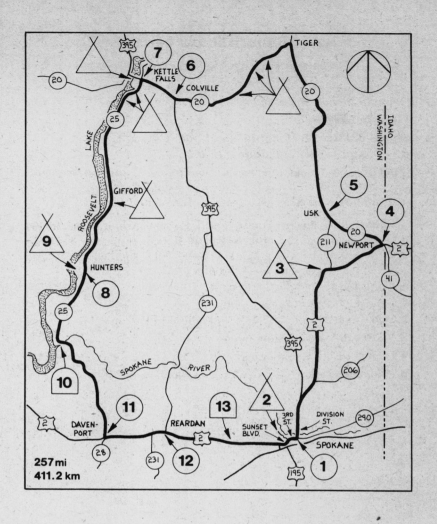

Mount Rainier Climb (#73)

PIERCE COUNTY, WASHINGTON

Length: *20 miles one way*

Terrain: *Very Hilly*

Points of Interest: *Mount Rainier National Park, Kautz Mud Flow, Visitor Center at Paradise, hiking*

Special Note: *avoid this trip on holidays and summer weekends when park traffic is heavy; for more information write Mount Rainier National Park, Ashford, WA 98304.*

1 Start at the Lodge Youth Hostel/Box 86, Ashford, WA 98304; ¼-mile west of the Nisqually Entrance to Mount Rainier National Park on Route 706; 90 miles southeast of Seattle; starting elevation is 2,000 ft.
Go east on Route 706 into park

2 Sunshine Point Campground
Continue 20-mile, 3,500-foot climb up to Paradise

3 Longmire/Park Visitor Center

4 Couger Rock Campground

5 Paradise/Park Visitor Center; elevation is 5,500 ft.

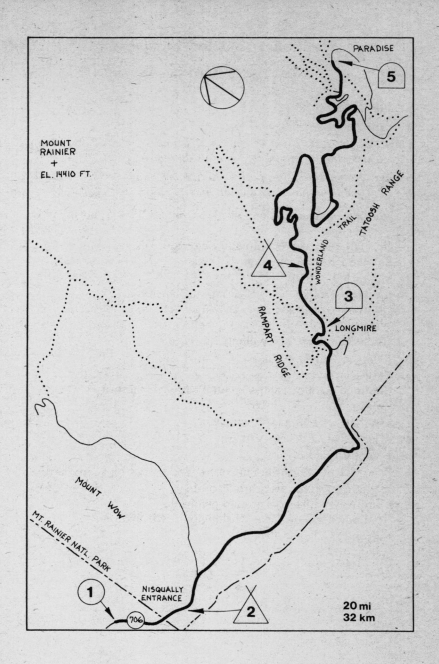

MOUNT
RAINIER
+
EL. 14410 FT.

PARADISE

5

TATOOSH RANGE

WONDERLAND TRAIL

4

3

LONGMIRE

RAMPART RIDGE

MOUNT WOW

MT. RAINIER NATL. PARK

NISQUALLY
ENTRANCE

1

706

2

20 mi
32 km

219

Southeast Seattle Tour (#74)

SEATTLE, WASHINGTON

Length: *17 miles*

Terrain: *Hilly*

Points of Interest: *parks of southeast Seattle, views of downtown Seattle and Mt. Rainier, Lake Washington.*

Special Note: *watch for potholes on some city streets; Seattle is accessible by plane, train, and bus.*

1 Start at Coleman Park on Lake Washington Blvd. S. north of Mt. Baker
 Go south on Lake Washington Blvd. S. Bikeway
 R–Lake Park Drive/uphill

2 Mount Baker Park
 R then L–Mount Baker Blvd. at McClellan St.
 Cross steep overpass ramp at Rainier Av./descend carefully
 West on Winthrop
 L–Cheasty Blvd./steep climb up Beacon Hill

3 Jefferson Park Golf Course
 L–Beacon Av.
 Continue on 39th/steep downhill with hairpin turn
 Continue on Carkeek Dr.
 Continue east on S. Henderson St.

4 Atlantic City-Beer Sheva Park
 L–Seward Park Av.

5 Seward Park/Kwanson cherry trees, a formal Japanese garden, and a fish hatchery are featured
 Continue on bike trail around peninsula
 Continue north on Lake Washington Blvd. Bikeway
 Return to Coleman Park

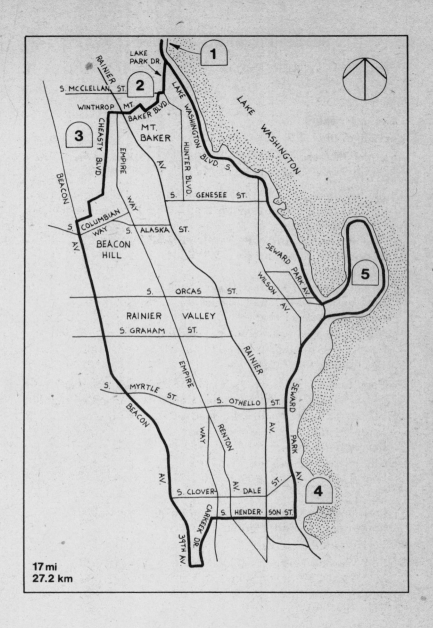

LAKE PARK DR.

RAINIER

S. McCLELLAN ST.

WINTHROP

MT.

BAKER BLVD.

CHEASTY BLVD.

MT. BAKER

BEACON

EMPIRE AV.

LAKE WASHINGTON BLVD. S.

HUNTER BLVD.

LAKE WASHINGTON

S. GENESEE ST.

WAY

S. COLUMBIAN WAY

AV.

BEACON HILL

S. ALASKA ST.

SEWARD PARK AV.

WILSON AV.

S. ORCAS ST.

RAINIER VALLEY

S. GRAHAM ST.

RAINIER

EMPIRE

WAY

S. MYRTLE ST.

BEACON

S. OTHELLO ST.

SEWARD PARK AV.

AV.

RENTON

WAY

AV.

S. CLOVER- DALE ST.

CARKEEK DR.

S. HENDER- SON ST.

39TH AV.

17 mi
27.2 km

221

Seattle–Puget Sound Tour (#75)

KING, KITSAP, JEFFERSON, ISLAND, AND SNOHOMISH COUNTIES, WASHINGTON

Length: *145 miles*

Terrain: *Rolling Hills*

Points of Interest: *Seattle, Fort Flagler State Park, Fort Worden State Park, San Juan Islands, island ferries*

1 Start at State Ferry Terminal/exit from I-5 to Seattle waterfront via Madison or Columbia Sts.; Seattle is served by bus, train, & plane
Take ferry to Winslow (Bainbridge Island)
Continue on Route 305 from Winslow
R (north)–Route 3
L (west)–Route 104/cross Hood Canal
R–to Beaver Valley and Chimacum
Continue north to Hadlock
R–at Hadlock to Marrowstone Island & Fort Flagler State Park
Second L–cross Indian Island to Marrowstone Island

2 Fort Flagler State Park

3 Fort Flagler Hostel/Fort Flagler State Park, Norland, WA 98358; go straight past ranger office, hostel is first building on left past open field; food services four miles away in Norland
Return to Hadlock
Continue straight through Hadlock
Bear R at fork–north to Route 20
North on Route 20 to Port Townsend

4 Port Townsend/ferry & bus service; food services; bike shop
Follow signs to Fort Worden State Park

5 Fort Worden State Park

6 Fort Worden Hostel/Fort Worden State Park, Port Townsend, WA 98368; the hostel is 600 feet behind park office
Return to Port Townsend
Take ferry to Whidbey Island
Continue on Route 20
R (south)–Route 525

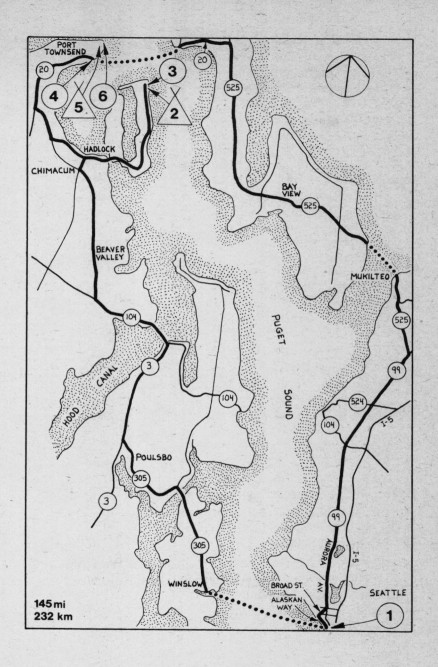

PORT
TOWNSEND

20

4   5   6   3

2

525

HADLOCK

CHIMACUM

20

BAY
VIEW

525

BEAVER
VALLEY

MUKILTEO

104

525

3

99

104

PUGET

524

I-5

HOOD

CANAL

SOUND

104

POULSBO

305

3

AURORA   I-5

99

305

WINSLOW

BROAD ST.

ALASKAN
WAY

AV.

SEATTLE

1

145 mi
232 km

Take ferry to Mukilteo
Continue south on Route 525
R (south)–Route 99
Continue into downtown Seattle (Aurora Av. N.)/watch city
   traffic
Bear R–onto Broad St./pass Seattle Center to waterfront
L–Alaskan Way
Return to State Ferry Terminal

CHAPTER ELEVEN

Southwest

Taos–Sangre De Cristo Mountains Tour (#76)

TAOS AND COLFAX COUNTIES, NEW MEXICO

Length: *100 miles*

Terrain: *Hilly to Very Hilly*

Points of Interest: *Taos, Elizabethtown, Red River Pass, Rio Grande Gorge Bridge*

Special Notes: *this is a rugged tour with elevations ranging from 7,000 ft. to over 9,800 ft.; although days can be warm, nights can be cold; to avoid snow, ride this tour between early June and late September; sudden storms are common.*

1 Start in Taos/bus service; motels; food services
   Go east on US 64/gradual climb, then very steep before pass
2 Palo Flechado Pass (el. 9,107 ft.)
   Steep downhill with sharp turns from pass to Route 38 jct.
3 Eagle Nest/motels; food services
   Continue north on Route 38/gradual uphill
4 Elizabethtown/old gold & copper mining town that burned in 1903
   Route 38 becomes steep up to Red River Pass
5 Red River Pass (el. 9,854 ft.)
   Steep and winding downhill follows
6 Red River/motels; food services
7 Questa/motels; food services
   L (south)–Route 3
   R (west)–US 64/7 miles to Rio Grande Gorge Bridge
8 Rio Grande Gorge Bridge
   Return on US 64 and continue south
   Return to Taos

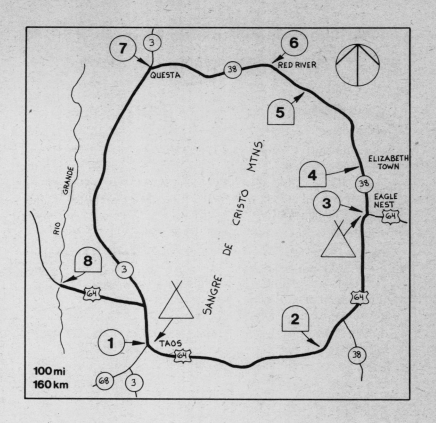

Albuquerque–Sante Fe Tour (#77)

BERNALILLO, SANTA FE, AND SANDOVAL COUNTIES, NEW MEXICO

Length: *204 miles*

Terrain: *Hilly*

Points of Interest: *University of New Mexico, Yemez State Monument, Santa Fe*

Special Notes: *this is a rugged tour with elevations reaching almost 10,000 feet; to avoid snow, take this tour between late May and early October; days here are hot and dry while nights may be 30 to 40 degrees cooler; carry extra water.*

1 Start at Canterbury Youth Hostel in Albuquerque/111 Stanford SE, Albuquerque, NM 87106; plane, train, & bus service; food services; bike shops; Univ. of New Mexico

Go north on Stanford

L–Central Av.

R–University Blvd.

L–Grand Av.

Continue on Marquette Av. after crossing over RR tracks

R–6th St.

L–Lomas Blvd.

R–San Pasquale into Old Town & the Plaza

Continue west from the Plaza

R–Rio Grande Blvd. (Route 194)

L–Corrales Rd. (Route 46)/cross Rio Grande; use caution on bridge

Straight on Route 528 at Coors Rd./uphill

L–Route 44/uphill

R–Route 4 at San Ysidro/hard uphills begin

2 San Ysidro/motel; food services

3 Jemez Springs/motel; food services

Bear L on road to Los Alamos

4 Los Alamos/motels; food services

Continue east and rejoin Route 4

R (south)–US 285 at Pojoaque

5 Pojoaque/motel; food services

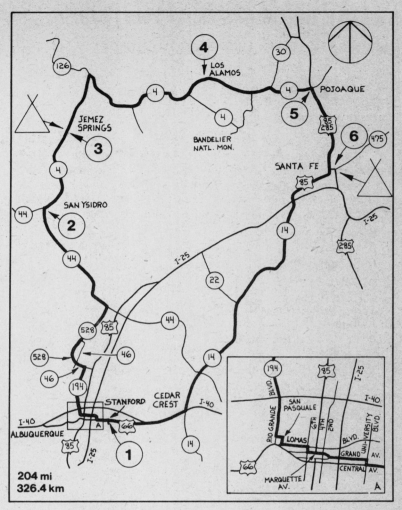

6 Santa Fe/motels; food services; New Mexico State Capitol;
Palace of the Governors (1620)
Continue south on US 85 (Cerrillous Rd.)
Continue onto Route 14
R–on frontage road along I-40
Continue west on Central Av. (US 66)
Return to Canterbury Youth Hostel

Rio Grande Valley Tour (#78)

BERNALILLO AND VALENCIA COUNTIES, NEW MEXICO

Length: *50 miles*
Terrain: *Level to Rolling Hills*
Points of Interest: *University of New Mexico, Rio Grande*

1 Start at the Univ. of New Mexico in Albuquerque/plane, train,
    & bus service; Canterbury Youth Hostel, 111 Standford SE,
    Albuquerque, NM 87106; food services; bike shops
  Go east on Central Av.
  R–Washington
  L–Zuni (Coal) Rd.
  R–San Mateo Blvd.
  R–Gibson Blvd.
  L–Broadway Blvd.
  R–Rio Bravo Blvd.
  L–Isleta Blvd. (US 85) to Isleta Pueblo
  L–to Route 47/cross Rio Grande
  R–Route 47
  R–Route 49 to Los Lunas
  R–US 85
  R–through Isleta Pueblo and across Rio Grande
  L–Route 47/becomes hilly
  Continue on Broadway Blvd.
  R–Stadium
  L–Yale Blvd.
  R–Central Av.
  Return to Univ. of New Mexico

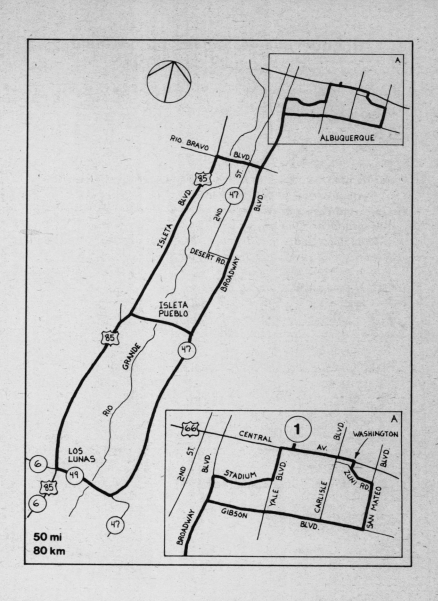

50 mi
80 km

Albuquerque–Gran Quivira National Monument Tour (#79)

BERNALILLO, TORRANCE, AND VALENCIA COUNTIES, NEW MEXICO

Length: *204 miles*

Terrain: *Rolling Hills to Hilly*

Points of Interest: *University of New Mexico, Manzano Mountains, Gran Quivira National Monument*

Special Notes: *this trip can be shortened by 50 miles if you omit side trip to Gran Quivira Natl. Monument; days here are hot and dry, while nights may be 30 to 40 degrees cooler; carry extra water; food stores may be closed on Sunday.*

1 Start at Canterbury Youth Hostel in Albuquerque/111 Stanford SE, Albuquerque, NM 87106; plane, train, & bus service; food services; bike shops; Univ. of New Mexico
Go north on Stanford
R–Central Av. (US 66)/watch traffic
Take frontage road at mouth of Tijeras Canyon along I-40
R–Route 14
R–continue on Route 14 at jct. with Route 55

2 Quarai State Monument

3 Mountainair/motels; food services
Continue south on Route 14 for 25 miles to Gran Quivira Natl. Monument

4 Gran Quivira Natl. Monument/early Indian & Spanish settlement
Return to Mountainair
L (west)–US 60

5 Abo State Monument
R–Route 6

6 Belen/motels; food services
R (north)–Route 6 & US 85

7 Camping at small park just south of Los Lunas
R–cross Rio Grande to Route 47 at intersection where Route 6 leaves US 85

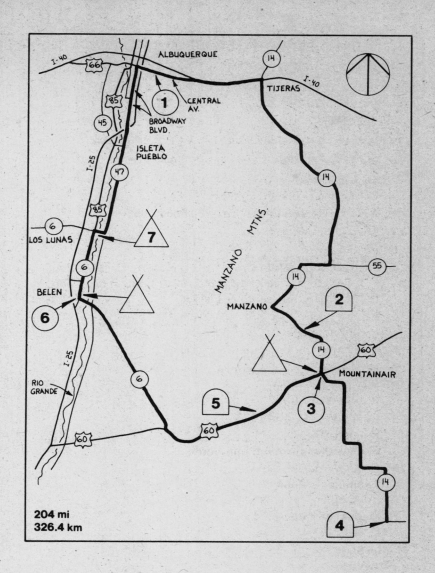

L–Route 47

Straight on Broadway Blvd. where Route 47 turns L on Desert Rd.

R–Central Av.

Return to Canterbury Youth Hostel

Central Arizona Tour (#80)

YAVAPAI AND COCONINO COUNTIES, ARIZONA

Length: *180 miles*
Terrain: *Hilly*
Points of Interest: *Sedona, Oak Creek Canyon, Flagstaff*
Special Note: *Flagstaff is an alternate starting point.*

Start in Cottonwood on US 89A southwest of Flagstaff
Go north on US 89A/uphill to Flagstaff

1 Food services/4 miles north of Sedona
2 Manzanita Campgrounds
3 Food services
4 Flagstaff/train & bus service; Weatherford Hostel, 23 N. Leroux, Flagstaff, AZ 86001; food services; bike shop
R–Lake Mary Rd./south of Flagstaff
5 Food services
R–Mormon Lake Rd.
6 Rainy Spring Campground
7 Double Springs Campground
8 Mormon Lake Lodge
R–Lake Mary Rd.
9 Clints Well/food services
R–Route 87
R–unmarked road to Camp Verde
10 Camp Verde/bus service; food services
Continue on Route 279
L–US 89A
Return to Cottonwood

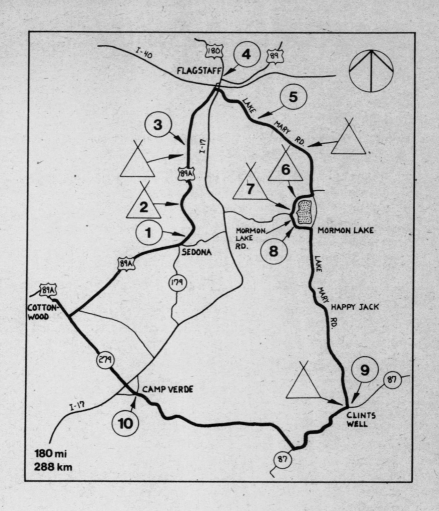

Carson Valley (#81)

DOUGLAS COUNTY, NEVADA

Length: *40 miles*

Terrain: *Level*

Points of Interest: *Mormon Station State Park, Genoa, ranches, wildlife areas*

1   Start at Mormon Station State Park on Route 206 south of Carson
    City
    Go north on Route 206 (Jacks Valley Road)
2   Genoa/Nevada's oldest town
    R (south)–US 395/watch traffic
    Bear R–continue south on Route 88
    R–Route 206
    Return to Mormon Station State Park

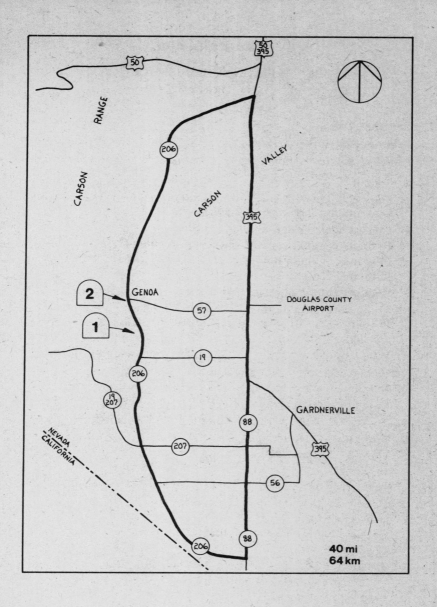

Rocky Mountain Tour (#82)

BOULDER, GILPIN, AND LARIMER COUNTIES, COLORADO

Length: *119.5 miles*
Terrain: *Hilly to Very Hilly*
Points of Interest: *University of Colorado, Rocky Mountain National Park, Longs Peak*

1. Start at Boulder Hostel/1107 12th St., Boulder, CO 80302; bus service; food services; bike shops
   Go east on College Av.
   R–Broadway at University of Colorado Campus
   Continue south on Route 93
   R–Route 72/begin 12-mile uphill

2. Wondervu/food services
   Continue west on Route 72/several switchbacks
   R–continue north on Routes 72 & 119/uphill followed by downhill

3. Nederland/Nederland Hostel, 1005 Jackson, P.O. Box 391, Nederland, CO 80466; food services
   Continue north on Route 72 (Peak to Peak Hwy.)
   L–Route 7 at Raymond/uphill to Wind River Pass

4. Rocky Mtn. Natl. Park and Longs Peak (el. 14,256 ft.)

5. Wind River Pass (el. 9,160 ft.)
   Downhill to Estes Park
   L–US 36
   L–Bus. US 34

6. Estes Park/motels; food services; bike shop
   R–McGregor Av.
   Continue on Devil's Gulch Rd.
   R–at sign to hostel

7. H-Bar-G Ranch Hostel/3500 H-Bar-G Rd., Box 1260, Estes Park, CO 80517; 6 miles NE of town
   Return to Estes Park
   East on US 36 and Route 66/uphill followed by downhill

8. Pinewood Springs/food services
   R–US 36 (Foothills Hwy.) after Lyons/hilly

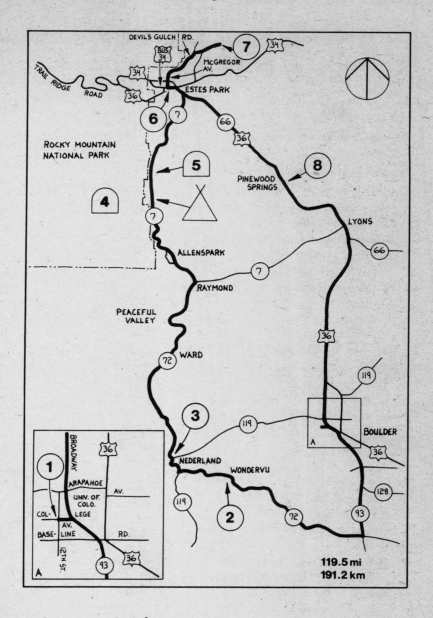

DEVILS GULCH RD.

BUS 34

McGREGOR AV.

34

TRAIL RIDGE ROAD

36

ESTES PARK

⑦ 34

⑥ ⑦

66

36

ROCKY MOUNTAIN NATIONAL PARK

⑤

④

⑧

PINEWOOD SPRINGS

⑦

LYONS

66

ALLENSPARK

⑦

RAYMOND

PEACEFUL VALLEY

36

72 WARD

119

③

119

BOULDER

A

36

NEDERLAND

WONDERVU

119

②

72

128

93

BROADWAY

36

①

ARAPAHOE

UNIV. OF COLO. AV.

COL-LEGE

BASE-LINE AV.

RD.

12TH ST.

A

93

36

119.5 mi
191.2 km

Continue on Broadway
Return to Boulder Hostel

Trail Ridge Road (#83)

LARIMER AND GRAND COUNTIES, COLORADO

Length: *50 miles one way*

Terrain: *Very Hilly*

Points of Interest: *Rocky Mountain National Park, Continental Divide*

Special Notes: *it always rains or snows on Trail Ridge Road in the afternoon; avoid peak tourist periods.*

1 Start at Estes Park Hostel/3500 H-Bar-G Rd., Box 1260, Estes Park, CO 80517; 6 miles NE of town
  Go west from hostel
  L–Devil's Gulch Rd.
  Continue on McGregor Av.

2 Estes Park/food services; bike shop
  R (west)–Bus. US 34 to Fall River Entrance, Rocky Mtn. Natl. Park
  Continue on Trail Ridge Rd./steady 20-mile climb; the road crests at 12,183 feet before descending to Grand Lake

3 Alpine Visitor Center
  Continue on Trail Ridge Road to Grand Lake

4 Grand Lake/food services
  L–Tunnel Rd.

5 Shadowcliff Youth Hostel/Box 658, Grand Lake, CO 80447

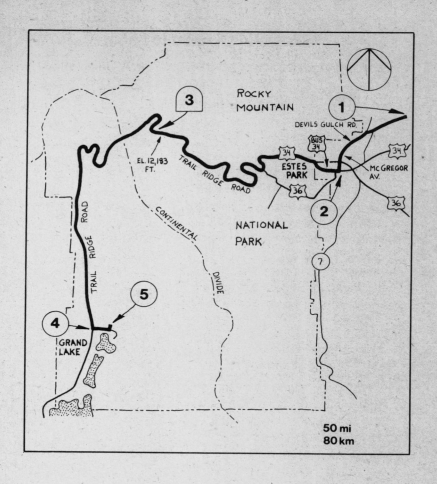

ROCKY MOUNTAIN

1

DEVILS GULCH RD.

BUS 34

34

ESTES PARK

McGREGOR AV.

34

3

EL. 12,183 FT.

TRAIL RIDGE ROAD

36

36

2

NATIONAL PARK

CONTINENTAL

DIVIDE

7

TRAIL RIDGE ROAD

5

4

GRAND LAKE

50 mi
80 km

Colorado Aspencade (#84)

ARCHULETA, LA PLATA, SAN JUAN, OURAY, MONTROSE,
GUNNISON, SAGUACHE, AND MINERAL COUNTIES,
COLORADO

Length: *401 miles*

Terrain: *Hilly to Very Hilly*

Points of Interest: *Rocky Mountains, Silverton-Durango Scenic Railroad, Saguache County Museum*

Special Notes: *this is a rugged seven-day mountain tour; this tour is recommended for late September when fall colors are at their peak; reservations are recommended for motels on this tour.*

1   Start at Pagosa Springs/bus service; motels (the Pagosa Spring Inn allows parking of cars); food services
    Go west on US 160/three-mile climb with good shoulder

2   Chimney Rock/food services

3   Bayfield/food services

4   Durango/bus service; motels; The Durango Hostel, P.O. Box 1445, 543 E. 2nd Av., Durango, CO 81301; food services; bike shop; scenic railroad
    North on US 550/seven-mile climb to Purgatory Ski Area
    Tough six-mile climb over Coal Bank Pass
    Two-mile downhill on rough pavement
    Five-mile climb over Molas Pass

5   Molas Pass (el. 10,910 ft.)
    Seven-mile downhill to Silverton

6   Silverton/motels; Teller House Youth Hostel, Box 457, Silverton, CO 81433; food services
    Continue north on US 550/ten-mile climb over Red Mtn. Pass

7   Red Mountain Pass (el. 11,018 ft.)
    Fourteen-mile steep downhill with a short tunnel
    Downhill into Ouray is very steep with tight switchbacks

8   Ouray/motels; food services; hot spring pool

9   Montrose/motels; food services
    East on US 50/four-mile climb to Cerro Summit
    Two-mile downhill

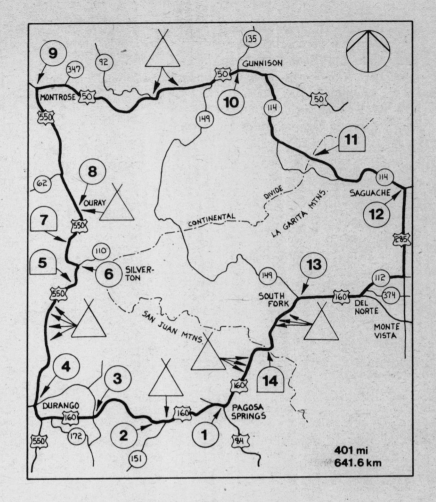

Four-mile climb to Blue Mesa Summit

10 Gunnison/motels; food services
Continue east on US 50 for eight miles
R (south)—Route 114/uphill to North Pass

11 North Pass (el. 10,149 ft.)

12 Saguache/motels (Sagauche Hotel); food services; county
museum
R (south)—US 285

R–Route 112 to Del Norte
Continue west on US 160

13 South Fork/motels; food services
Long climb over Wolf Creek Pass/snow tunnel just before summit

14 Wolf Creek Pass (el. 10,850 ft.)
Return to Pagosa Springs

CHAPTER TWELVE
California

Volcanic Venture (#85)

SHASTA, LASSEN, TEHAMA, AND PLUMAS COUNTIES,
CALIFORNIA

Length: *170 miles*

Terrain: *Very Hilly*

Points of Interest: *Lassen Volcanic National Park, lava flows, thermal areas, fishing, hiking.*

Special Notes: *elevations on this trip vary from 4,000 to 8,500 feet, so give your body time to acclimate; for a good bicycle map of this area write Bicycle Coordinator, District 2, Planning Dept., P.O. Box 2107, Redding, CA 96001.*

1 Start in Susanville off US 395 in northeastern California/bus service; food services; bike shop; no food services for next 51 miles.
   Go west on Route 36
   Bear R—Route 44
   L—Routes 44 & 89

2 Old Station/food services
   L—continue south on Route 89 to Lassen Volcanic National Park/entrance fee

3 Manzanita Lake/food services; there are several other campsites in the park
   Begin 3000-foot climb to roadway summit (el. 8,512 ft.)

4 Lassen Peak (el. 10,457 ft.)/dormant volcano
   R—at jct. with Route 36 to Mineral

5 Mineral/food services
   L—Route 172

6 Mill Creek/food services
   R—Routes 36 & 89
   R—Route 89/continue along south shore of Lake Almanor; food services
   Cross Feather River
   L—Route 147
   R—Route 36 at Clear Creek

7 Westwood/food services; bike shop
   Return to Susanville

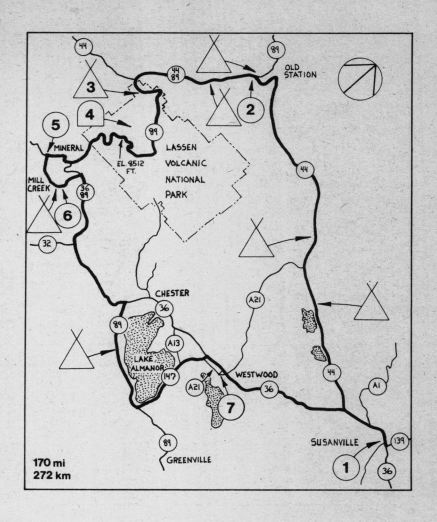

170 mi
272 km

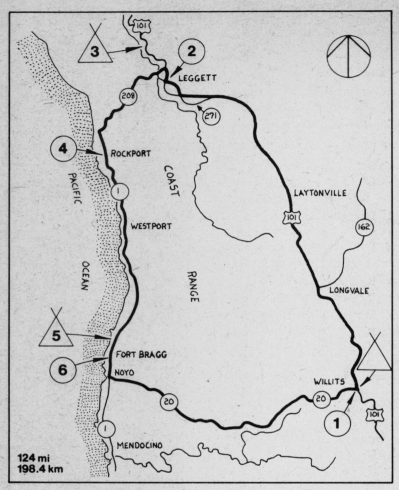

Northern California Coast (#86)

Northern California Coast (#86)

MENDOCINO COUNTY, CALIFORNIA

Length: *124 miles*
Terrain: *Hilly to Very Hilly*
Points of Interest: *California coast, Georgia-Pacific Museum in Fort Bragg, Noyo Harbor.*
Special Note: *watch for logging trucks on Route 1.*

1 Start at Willits on US 101 north of Ukiah/motel; food services
   Go north on US 101/two and four-lane hwy with 0-8 foot paved shoulder
2 Leggett/food services
3 Standish Hickey State Park
   L (west)–Route 208 to Route 1/two long climbs
   Continue south on Route 1
4 Rockport/food services
   Uphill south of Rockport
5 Mackerricher Beach State Park
6 Fort Bragg/motels; food services; museum
   L (east)–Route 20 at Noyo/several uphills
   Return to Willits

▽   ▽   ▽

Santa Rosa Terrible Two (#87)

SONOMA AND NAPA COUNTIES, CALIFORNIA

Length: *208 miles*
Terrain: *Very Hilly*
Points of Interest: *Napa Valley wine country, geysers, Stewart's Point Primitive Area, California coast, Fort Ross, Santa Rosa Apple Orchards*
Special Note: *this is an extremely hilly ride; cyclists should be in excellent shape.*

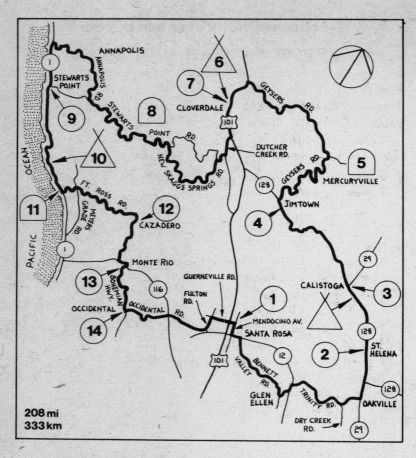

1 Start at the Bike Peddler in Santa Rosa on McConnell Av. just off Mendocino Av./bus service; motels; food services; bike shops

Go south on Mendocino Av.

L—Route 12

R—Bennett Valley Rd. to Glen Ellen

L—to Route 12 at Glen Ellen

L—Route 12

R—Trinity Rd. to Oakville; steep uphill and downhill

L—Route 29

2 St. Helena/food services

3 Calistoga/motels (Navies Hot Springs, 1614 Lincoln Av., and Dr. Wilkinson's Hot Springs, 1507 Lincoln Av., Calistoga, CA 94515); food services
Continue north on Route 128

4 Jimtown/food services
R–Geysers Rd/steep uphill to Mercuryville (el. 2,500 ft.), then downhill

5 Geysers
L–US 101

6 KOA Campground (26460 River Rd., Cloverdale, CA 95425)

7 Cloverdale/food services
R–Dutcher Creek Rd.
R–to New Skaggs Springs Rd., which detours and then rejoins Stewart's Point Rd./steep uphills and downhills

8 Stewart's Point Primitive Area
R–Annapolis Rd./uphill, followed by steep downhill
L–Route 1 (Coast Highway)

9 Stewart's Point/food services

10 Salt Point State Park

11 Fort Ross/old Russian-built fort
L–Fort Ross Rd./steep uphill

12 Cazadero/food services
R–to Route 116
L–Route 116
R–Bohemian Hwy./uphill follows

13 Monte Rio/food services

14 Occidental/food services
L–Occidental Rd./uphill, then downhill to Santa Rosa
L–Fulton Rd.
R–Guerneville Rd.
R–Mendocino Av.
Return to start

Point Reyes–Pacific Coast Tour (#88)

MARIN COUNTY, CALIFORNIA

Length: 59 *miles*

Terrain: *Very Hilly*

Points of Interest: *Point Reyes National Seashore, Stinson Beach, Samuel Taylor State Park, Pacific Ocean*

1 Start at Point Reyes Hostel/P.O. Box 247, Point Reyes Station, CA 94956; nine miles west of Olema off Limantour Road in Point Reyes Natl. Seashore
   R–Limantour Rd./extremely steep uphill
   R–to Olema

2 Olema/food services
   R (south)–Route 1

3 Stinson Beach/food services; beach
   L–Panoramic Hwy./steep uphill

4 Pan Toll Park
   L–out of Pan Toll Park to Ridgecrest Blvd.
   R–Bolinas Rd./steep downhill through Redwoods
   Cross Reservoir
   Climb hill
   Downhill to Fairfax

5 Fairfax/food services
   L–Sir Francis Drake Blvd./uphill, then level

6 Samuel Taylor State Park
   Continue on Sir Francis Drake Blvd. to Olema
   Return to Point Reyes Hostel

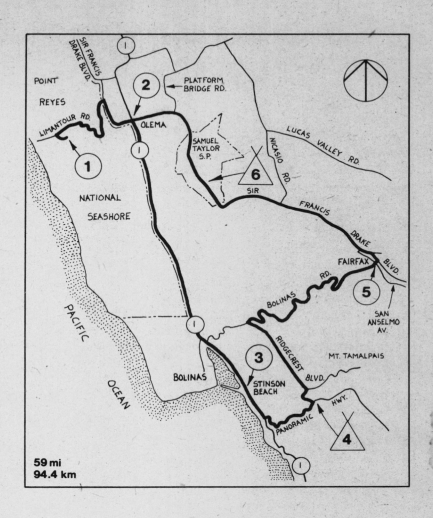

Pacific Ocean–San Francisco Bay (#89)

SAN FRANCISCO CITY AND MARIN COUNTY, CALIFORNIA

Length: *28 miles*

Terrain: *Level to Rolling Hills*

Points of Interest: *Golden Gate Park, Pacific waterfront, Lincoln Park, Golden Gate Bridge, Sausalito*

Special Notes: *this entire tour follows signed bicycle routes; San Francisco is accessible by bus, train, and plane.*

1   Start at Redwood Memorial Grove in Golden Gate Park
Go west on John F. Kennedy Dr.
Bear L–follow bike route signs to South Dr.
West on South Dr.
L–continue along Sunset Blvd./leave Golden Gate Park
L–Lake Merced Blvd.
Continue around Lake Merced
R–John Muir Dr.
Bear R–Skyline Blvd. (Route 35)
L–Park Rd.
Continue north along Great Hwy.
R–Point Lobos Av.
L–El Camino Del Mar
R–Clement St.
L–Legion of Honor Dr.

2   Lincoln Park
R–El Camino Del Mar
Continue on Lincoln Blvd.
L–follow bike route signs to Golden Gate Bridge

3   Golden Gate Bridge
Cross Golden Gate Bridge on right sidewalk
Loop under US 101 from Vista Point parking area through foot tunnel
L–Conzelman Rd./continue downhill
Continue on East Rd.
Follow waterfront streets into Sausalito

4   Sausalito/food services
Return to Golden Gate Bridge/uphill

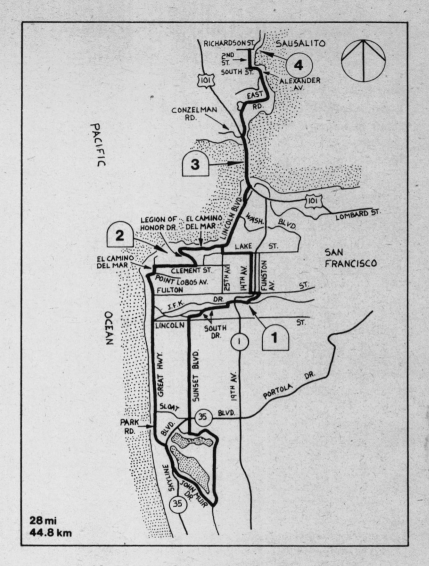

Cross Golden Gate Bridge on right sidewalk
Travel through parking lot to Lincoln Blvd.
R–Lincoln Blvd.
L–25th Av.
L–Lake St.
R–14th Av./cross Fulton St./return to Golden Gate Park

American River Bicycle Trail (#90)

SACRAMENTO COUNTY, CALIFORNIA

Length: *23 miles one way*

Terrain: *Level*

Points of Interest: *State Fair Grounds, American River Parkway, Nimbus Fish Hatchery, swimming*

Special Note: *for a trail map write Office of Bicycle Facilities, Division of Highways, P.O. Box 1499, Sacramento, CA 95807*

West end of trail is in Discovery Park, 1½ miles north of the center of Sacramento. East end of trail is at Nimbus Dam and Fish Hatchery. The route consists of a wide, well-maintained, blacktop off-road bicycle trail. The trail follows the American River through parklands that have mostly been maintained in their natural state. The trail is a popular local recreation-way, and can be very congested on weekends

1 Sacramento Hostel/P.O. Box 13907, Sacramento, CA 95813

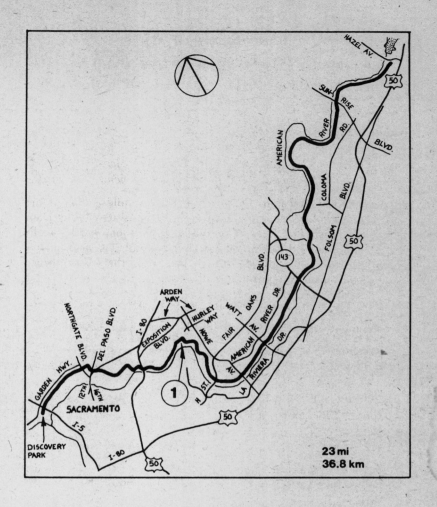

HAZEL AV.

50

SUN- RISE

AMERICAN

RIVER

RD.

BLVD.

COLOMA

BLVD.

FOLSOM

50

143

NORTHGATE BLVD.

ARDEN WAY

HURLEY WAY

DEL PASO BLVD.

I-80

EXPOSITION BLVD.

HOWE

WATT AV.

FAIR OAKS BLVD.

AMERICAN RIVER DR.

DR.

GARDEN HWY.

12TH

16TH

SACRAMENTO

AV.

H ST.

LA RIVIERA

①

I-5

50

DISCOVERY PARK

I-80

50

23 mi
36.8 km

Lake Tahoe (#91)

PLACER AND ELDORADO COUNTIES, CALIFORNIA
DOUGLAS, CARSON CITY, AND WASHOE COUNTIES,
NEVADA

Length: *72 miles*

Terrain: *Hilly to Very Hilly*

Points of Interest: *Lake Tahoe, Sierra Nevada Mountains, swimming beaches, flashy casinos in Nevada*

Special Notes: *traffic can be heavy on steep, narrow roads; best cycling time is in spring or fall; avoid holidays and weekends; elevations here are over 6,000 feet, so give your body time to acclimate; for a Lake Tahoe Bicycle Touring Guide write Office of Bicycle Facilities, Division of Highways, P.O. Box 1499, Sacramento, CA 95807.*

1 Start in South Lake Tahoe/bus service; motels; food services; bike shop
   Go south on US 50/busy 4-lane highway
   R–Route 89/steep, narrow 2-lane road with no shoulders
   Follow bike path from West Way to Forest Service Visitor Center
   Continue on Route 89
2 Emerald Bay State Park
3 D.L. Bliss State Park
4 Meeks Bay/food services
5 Sugar Pine Point State Park
   Follow bike path from Cherry St. to Tahoe City
6 Tahoe City/motel; food services
   Follow bike path north along Route 28
7 Tahoe Recreation Area
   Continue on Route 28 at Dollar Point/very steep hills
8 Tahoe Vista, Kings Beach, & Crystal Bay/motels; food services
9 Lake Tahoe–Nevada State Park/swimming
   R (south)–US 50/busy 4-lane highway
10 Nevada Beach Campground
   Return to South Lake Tahoe

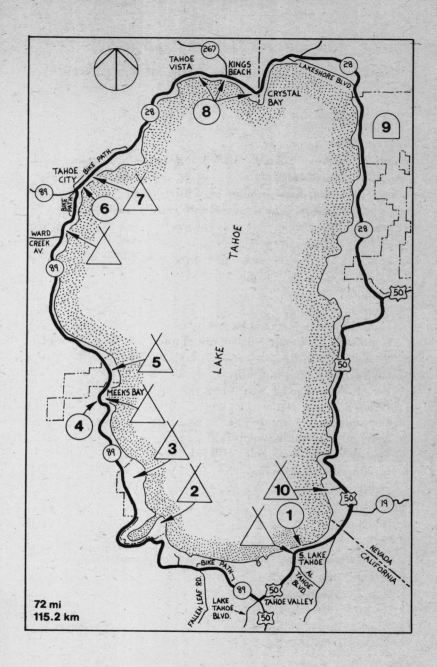

72 mi
115.2 km

Mariposa–Yosemite Tour (#92)

MARIPOSA, MADERA, AND TOULUMNE COUNTIES, CALIFORNIA

Length: *170.5 miles*
Terrain: *Hilly*
Points of Interest: *Yosemite Valley and Yosemite National Park, Sierra Nevada Mountains*
Special Note: *this tour presents some steep grades, narrow roads, and high traffic volumes; cycle with extreme care.*

1   Start at Mariposa 40 miles east of Merced on Route 140/bus
     service; motels; food services
     Go south on Route 49 (Boot Jack Rd.)
     Continue through Ahwahnee to Oakhurst

2   Oakhurst/food services
     L (north)–Route 41
     Enter Yosemite National Park
     Continue to Yosemite Village/use caution at Wawona Tunnel

3   Yosemite Village/food services
     Go west from Yosemite Village
     Bear R–New Big Oak Flat Rd/go through 3 tunnels
     Leave Yosemite National Park
     Continue west on Route 120
     L–Route J20 (Smith Station Rd.)
     Bear R–Route J20 (Greeley Hill Rd.)

4   Coulterville/food services
     L–Route 49
     Return to Mariposa

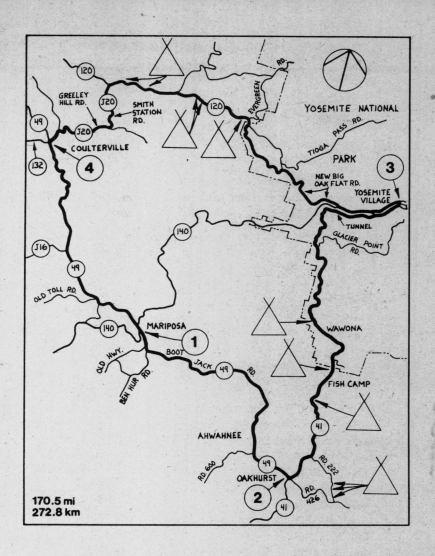

170.5 mi
272.8 km

Santa Barbara County Tour (#93)

SANTA BARBARA COUNTY, CALIFORNIA

Length: *125 miles*

Terrain: *Hilly*

Points of Interest: *Santa Barbara, University of California–Santa Barbara, Pacific Coast, Lake Cachuma, San Marcos Pass*

1 Start at Santa Barbara, northwest of Ventura on US 101/bus service; motels (Motel 6, 3505 State St., or Sandpiper Lodge, 3525 State St., Santa Barbara, CA 93105); food services; bike shop
   Go west on State St./becomes Hollister Av.
   L–Fairview Av.
   Continue to UCSB Campus

2 University of California–Santa Barbara
   Follow bike paths through campus to Isla Vista
   West on Colegio Rd.
   R–Stokes Rd.
   L–Hollister Av.
   Enter on-ramp to US 101

3 El Capitan Beach State Park

4 Refugio Beach State Park

5 Gaviota/food services

6 Gaviota Beach State Park
   L–Route 1 at Las Cruces
   Continue west on Ocean Av. into Lompoc

7 Lompoc/Motel 6 (1415 E. Ocean Av., Lompoc, CA 93436); food services
   East on Ocean Av.
   R–Route 1/uphill
   L–Santa Rosa Rd. to Buellton/climb along Santa Ynez River
   Continue on Route 246 to Solvang

8 Solvang/food services
   R–Route 154/long uphill climbs
   L–Old Stagecoach Rd.

9 San Marcos Pass (el. 2,225 ft.)
   Exit first off-ramp
   L–Cathedral Oaks

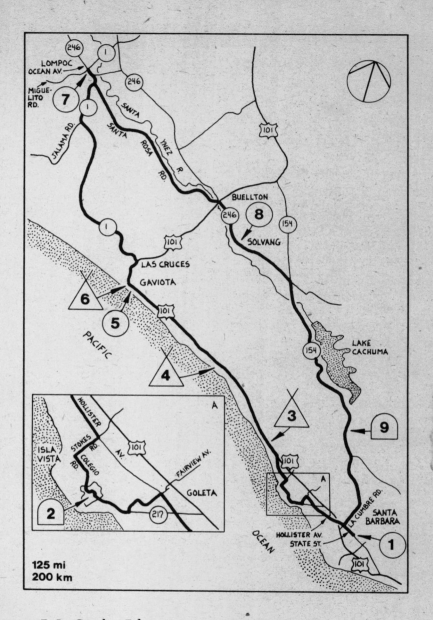

R–La Cumbre Rd.
L–State St.
Return to Santa Barbara

Fallbrook (#94)

SAN DIEGO COUNTY, CALIFORNIA

Length: *50 miles*

Terrain: *Hilly*

Points of Interest: *southern California countryside, rural cycling roads*

Special Note: *the best time to ride this tour is in spring or fall.*

1 Start at Pala Mesa Golf Club near Fallbrook, 40 miles north of San Diego off I-15 and US 395
  Go north on US 395
  Bear R–to Rainbow
  Continue north on Rainbow Canyon Rd.
  L–Pala Rd. to Rancho California
2 Rancho California/food services
  Return on Pala Rd. south to Pala
3 Pala Mission and Pala Indian Reservation
  R–Route 76
  R–Olive Hill Rd. at Bonsall
  R–Mission Rd.
  L–Live Oak Rd.
4 Live Oak County Park
  Return to Pala Mesa Golf Club

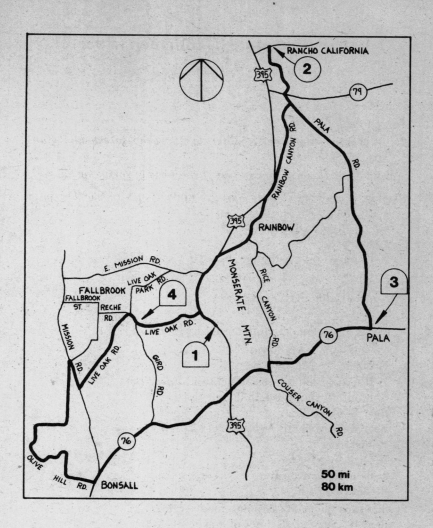

The Ride of the Gentlemen (#95)

SAN DIEGO COUNTY, CALIFORNIA

Length: *50 miles*
Terrain: *Hilly*
Points of Interest: *southern California vineyards, forested hills, and rugged mountains*
Special Note: *the best time to ride this tour is in spring or fall.*

1 Start at Felicita County Park, 30 miles north of San Diego off I-15 at 17th St.
   Go north on 17th St.
   L–Redwood
   R–County Route S-6 (Grand Av.) in Escondido
   L–Quince
   L–Washington
   R–Rock Springs Rd.
   Bear R–Borden Rd.
   Continue on Richland Rd.
   Continue onto Mulberry
   L–Olive
   L–Buena Creek Rd./past Pechstein Reservoir
   R–Monte Vista (or Foothill Dr.)
   Bear R–Foothill Dr.
   Bear R–Warmlands Av.
   R–Vista Way
   R–Ormsby St.
   L–Gopher Canyon Rd.
   R–Old River Rd.

2 San Luis Ray/halfway point; food services
   Bear R–Lilac Rd./3 miles of gravel into Lilac
   Bear R–Valley Center Rd. at Valley Center/watch traffic
   Continue on Bear Valley Rd.
   Continue on Eldorado Dr. at Route 78
   Continue onto 17th St.
   Return to Felicita County Park

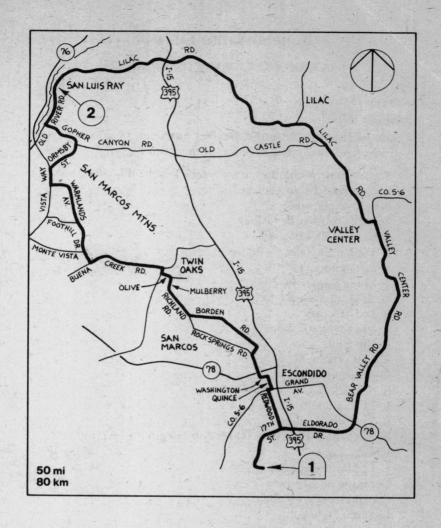

50 mi
80 km

Rancho Santa Fe (#96)

SAN DIEGO COUNTY, CALIFORNIA

Length: *18 miles*

Terrain: *Hilly*

Points of Interest: *beautiful Rancho Santa Fe (a 25-square-mile residential paradise 20 miles north of San Diego)*

1   Start at Ranch Santa Fe east of Solana Beach off I-5/food services
Go south on Paseo Delicias
Bear L–La Gracia
Continue on Via Del Alba
L–Calzada Del Bosque
R–Via De La Valle
R–Las Planideras
L–Linea Del Cielo
R–El Camino Real
R–Los Morros
R–Via Fortuna Rd.
L–San Elijo
Bear R–Via De La Cumbre
L–Av. De Acacias
R–San Elijo
L–El Montevideo Rd.
R–Via Fortuna Rd.
R–El Camino Del Norte/along San Dieguito Reservoir
R–Lago Linda
L–El Montevideo Rd.
Continue on El Vuelo
Continue on Las Colinas
L–Paseo Delicias
Return to Rancha Santa Fe

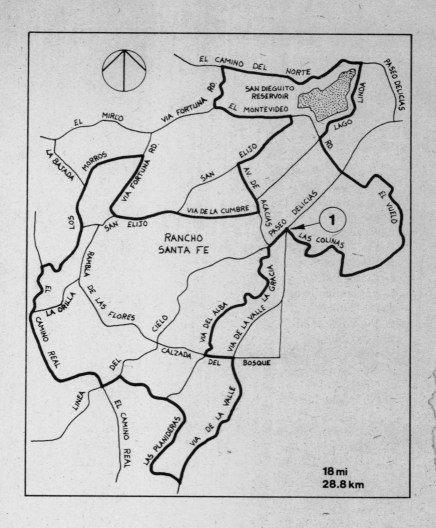

AYH MEMBERSHIP APPLICATION

AMERICAN YOUTH HOSTELS AREA COUNCILS

ALASKA COUNCIL
Box 1543
Juneau, AK 99802
(907) 766-2876

ARIZONA STATE
14049 North 38th Place
Phoenix, AZ 85032
(602) 992-6482

BOSTON (Greater)
251 Harvard Street
Brookline, MA 02146
(617) 731-6692

CENTRAL CALIFORNIA COUNCIL
P.O. Box 28148
San Jose, CA 95159
(408) 298-0670

CHICAGO (Metropolitan)
3712 North Clark
Chicago, IL 60613
(312) 327-8114

COLUMBUS
160 South Dawson Avenue
Columbus, OH 43209
(614) 846-3229

DELAWARE VALLEY
35 South 3rd Street
Philadelphia, PA 19103
(215) 925-6004

DETROIT (Metropolitan)
3024 Coolidge
Berkley, MI 48072
(313) 545-0511

ERIE-ANA
304 North Church Street
Bowling Green, OH 43402
(419) 352-1252

GOLDEN GATE
Building 240
Fort Mason
San Francisco, CA 94123
(415) 771-4646

HARTFORD AREA
P.O. Box 10392
West Hartford, CT 06110
(203) 247-6356

LIMA
Box 173
Lima, OH 45802
(419) 222-7301

LOS ANGELES
1502 Palos Verdes Drive, North
Harbor City, CA 90710
(213) 831-8847

MINNESOTA
475 Cedar Street
St. Paul, MN 55101
(612) 292-4126

NEBRASKALAND
12637 N. St.
Omaha, NE 68137
(402) 896-1402

NEW YORK (Metropolitan)
132 Spring Street
New York, NY 10012
(212) 431-7100

NORTHEAST IOWA
139 West Greene Street
Postville, IA 52162
(319) 864-7421

NORTHERN NEW YORK COUNCIL
42 West Main St. #3
Malone, NY 12953
(518) 358-2829

NORTHWEST INDIANA
8231 Lake Shore Drive
Gary IN 46403
(219) 938-1312

OREGON STATE COUNCIL
4218 S.W. Primrose St.
Portland, OR 97219
(503) 244-9016

OZARK AREA
5400 A Southwest
St. Louis, MO 63139
(314) 644-3560

PITTSBURGH
6300 Fifth Avenue
Pittsburgh, PA 15232
(412) 362-8181

POTOMAC AREA
1520 16th Street NW
Washington, DC 20036
(202) 462-5780

ROCKY MOUNTAIN
1107 12th Street
P.O. Box 2370
Boulder, CO 80302
(303) 442-9304

SAN DIEGO
1031 India Street
San Diego, CA 92101
(714) 239-2644

SYRACUSE
459 Westcott Street
Syracuse, NY 13210
(315) 472-5788

TOLEDO
3440 Lawrin Drive
Toledo, OH 43623
(419) 474-0267

TRI-STATE
5400 Lanius Lane
Cincinnati, OH 45224
(513) 541-1972

WESTERN MICHIGAN
1013 W. Burton
Grand Rapids, MI 49509
(616) 361-7106

WASHINGTON STATE
1431 Minor Avenue
Seattle, WA 98101
(206) 382-4180

WISCONSIN
7218 West North Avenue
Wauwatosa, WI 53213
(414) 257-2323

OR CALL AMERICAN YOUTH HOSTELS, National Campus—TOLL FREE **800-336-6019**
FOR AN AGENT NEAR YOU

FILL OUT AND RETURN

NOTE: Individual AYH membership cards are valid in 50 countries. All such memberships expire on Dec. 31st of the year issued, except that cards purchased in Oct., Nov. and Dec. of the year of issue will expire on Dec. 31st of the following year. Cards are not transferable and no refunds are given.

Return completed form with check or money order to:
a local office above, or to American Youth Hostels, 1332 I St. NW, Washington, D.C. 2005

I am ordering the:
☐ Junior Pass (17 yrs. and under) $7
☐ Senior Pass (18 yrs. to 59 yrs.) $14
☐ 3-Year Senior Pass (same ages) $35
☐ Senior Citizen Pass (60 yrs. and over) $7

☐ IYHF Handbook: Vol. I $6.00
☐ IYHF Handbook: Vol. II. $6.00
☐ Sheet-Sleep Sack $9.50
Total Enclosed $_____

Birth Date _____
mth/day/yr

Ms./Mr._____
last name   first name

Home Address_____
street

_____
city   state   zip
Mail Address (if different)_____

271